Lighthouse Seascapes
A Coloring Book for Adult Relaxation

Created by
Corinne Larsen

Lighthouse Seascapes
A Coloring Book for Adult Relaxation
Corinne Larsen
Larsen Falls Publishing

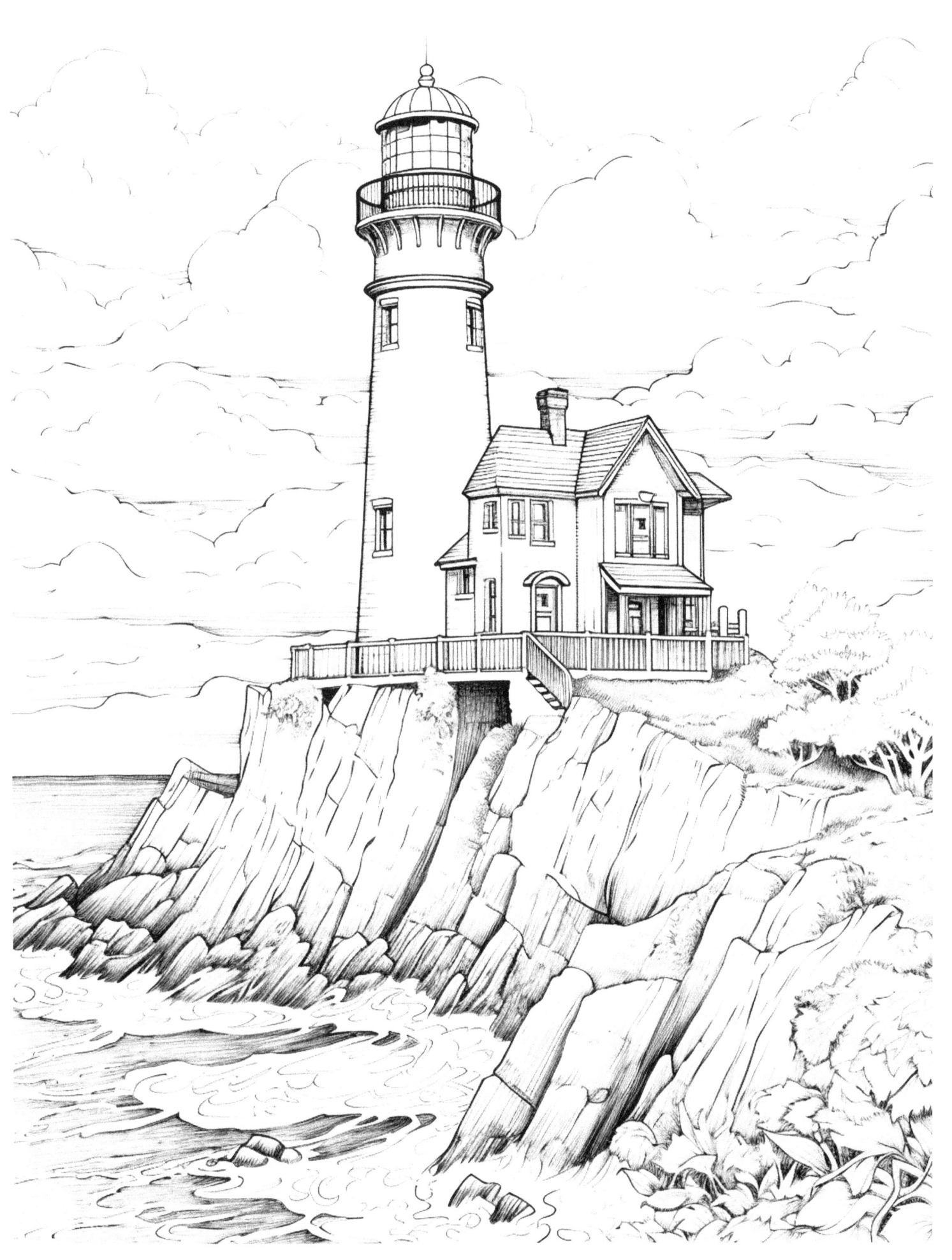

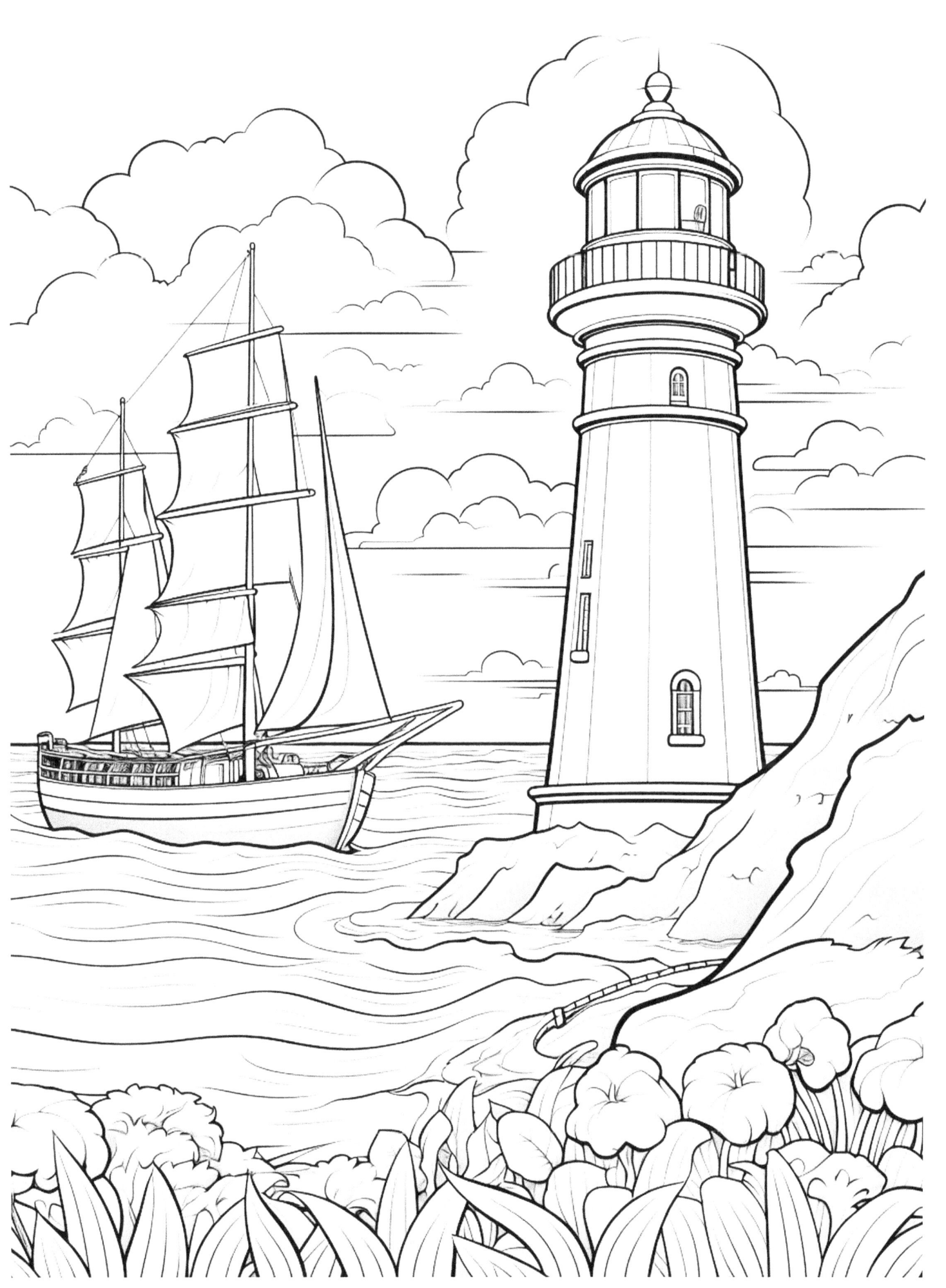

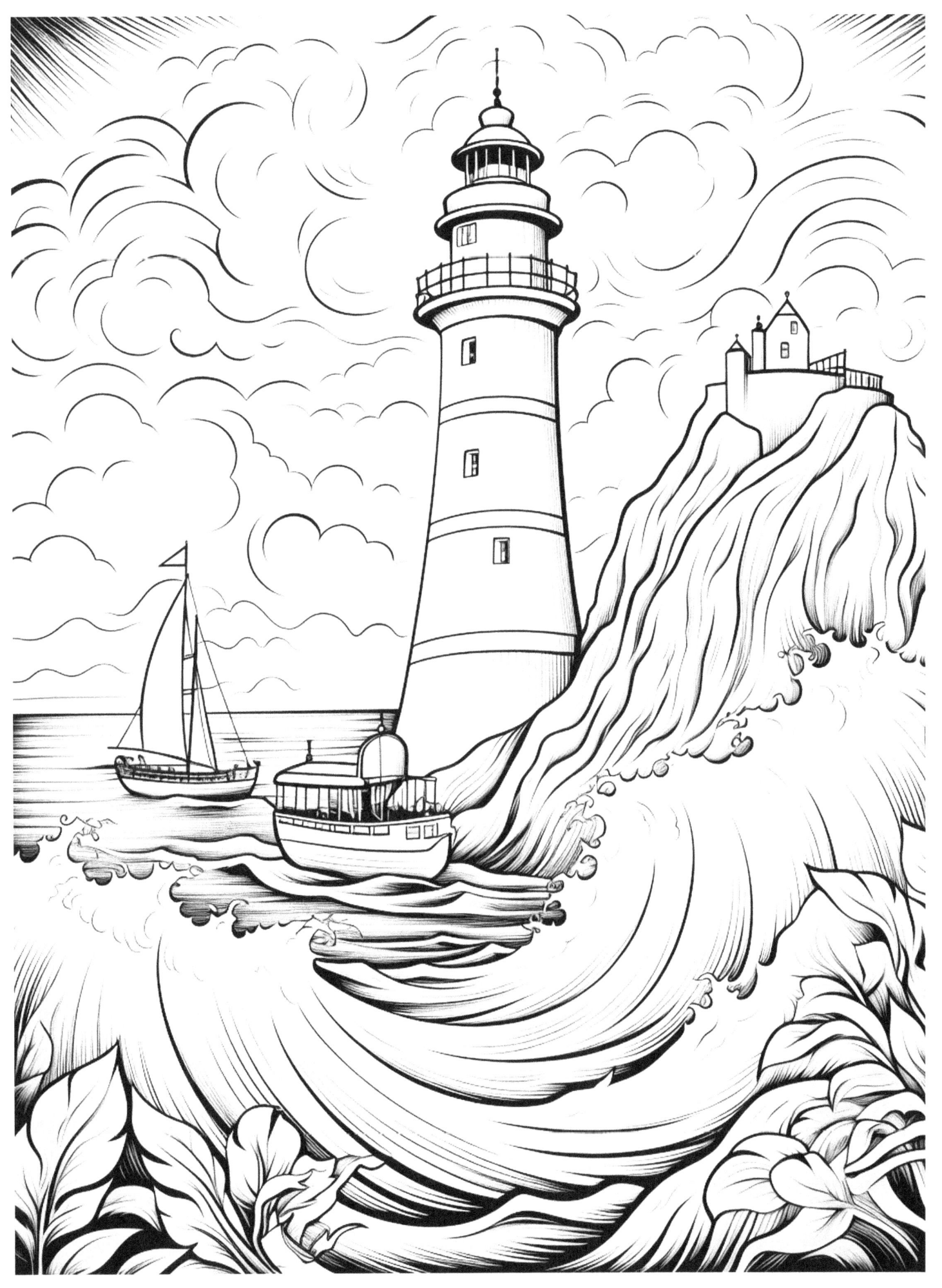

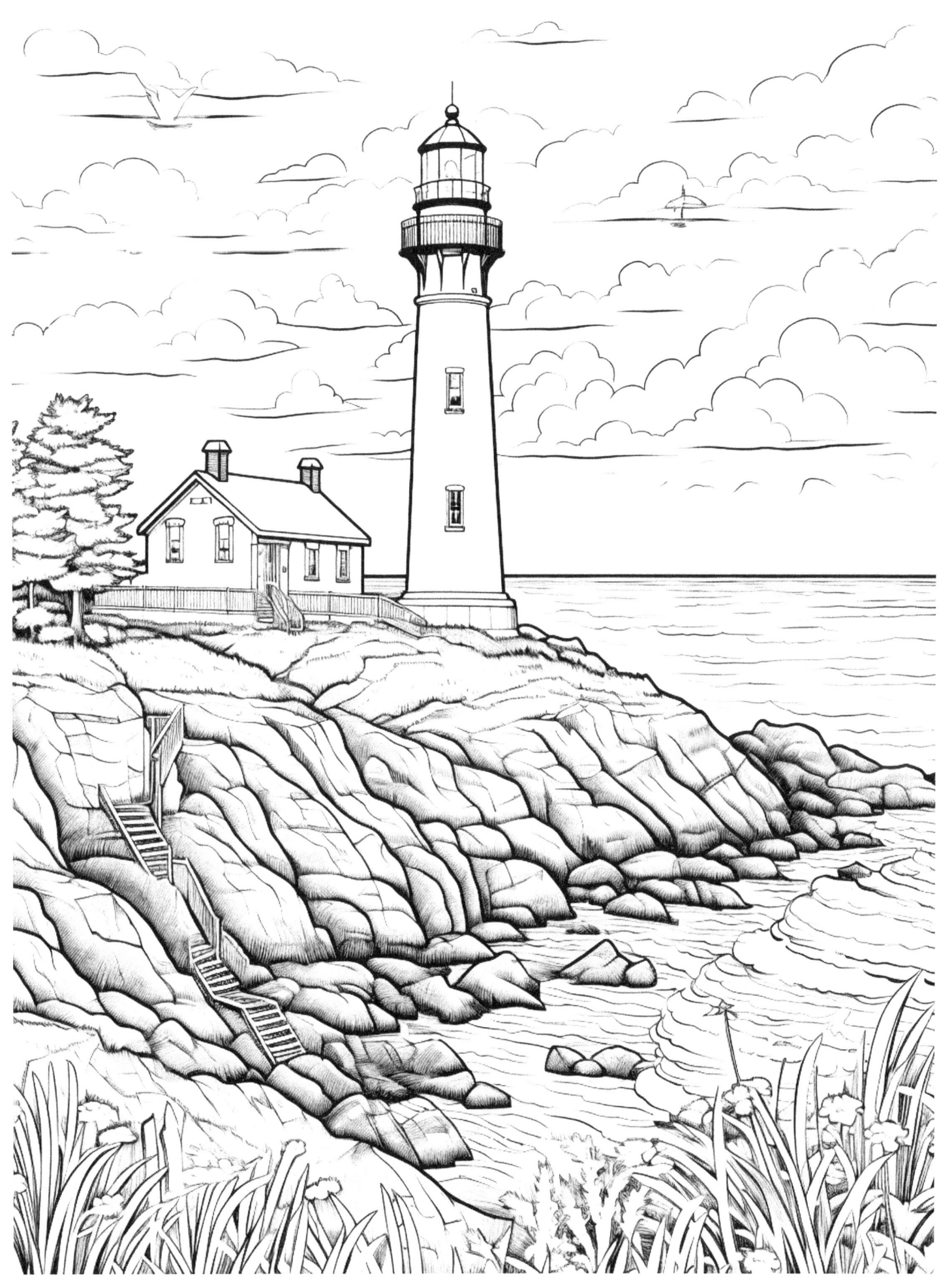

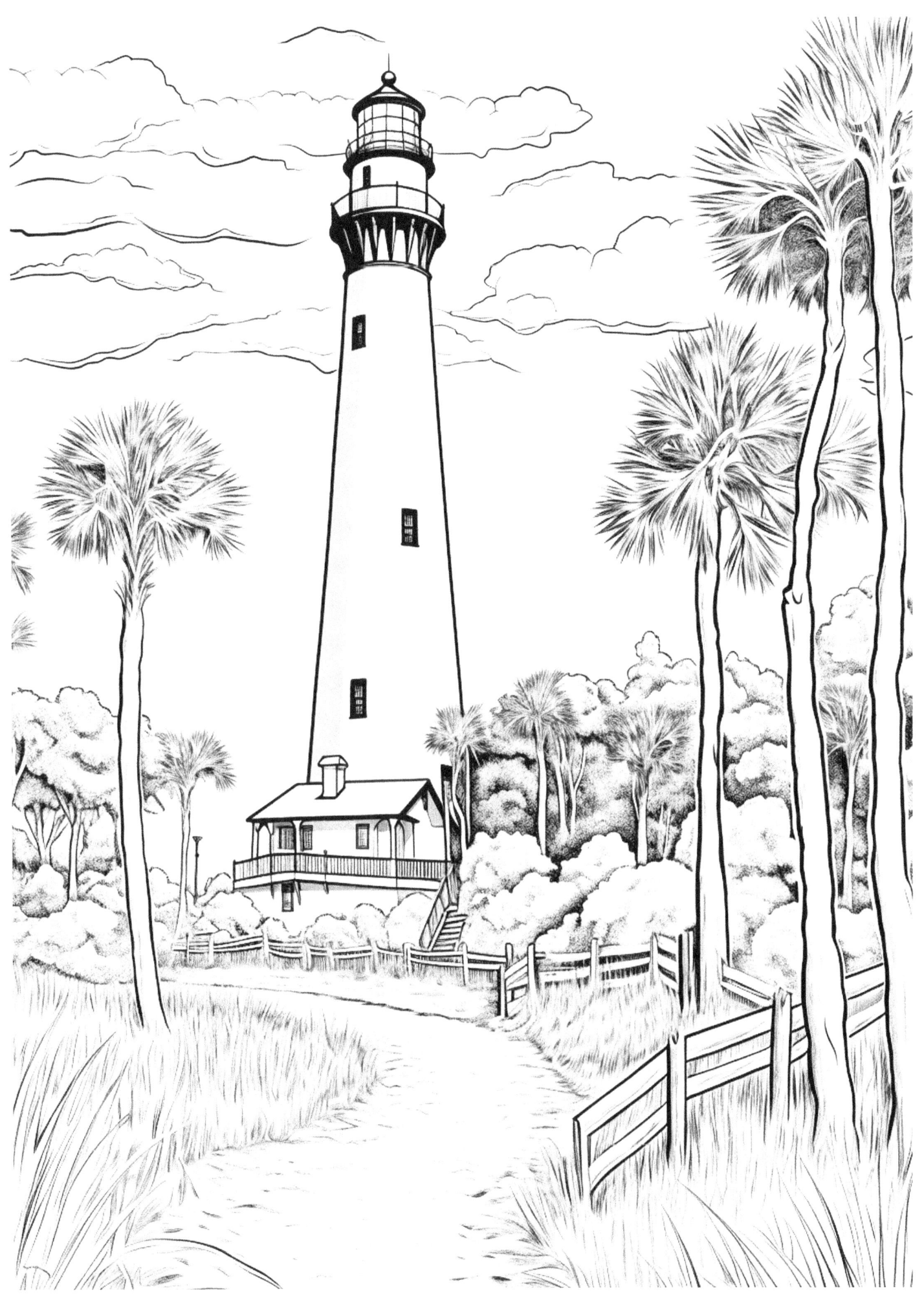

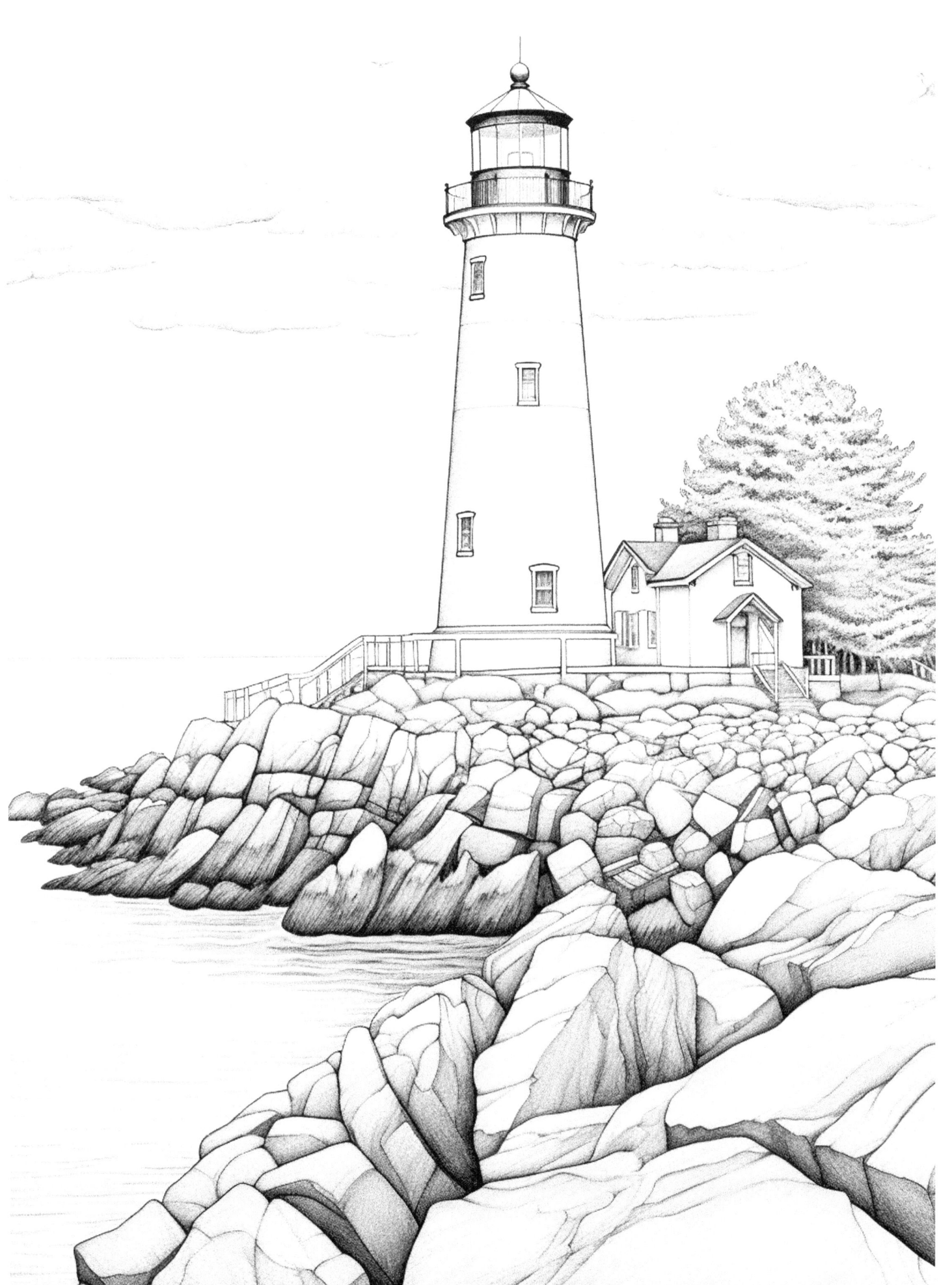

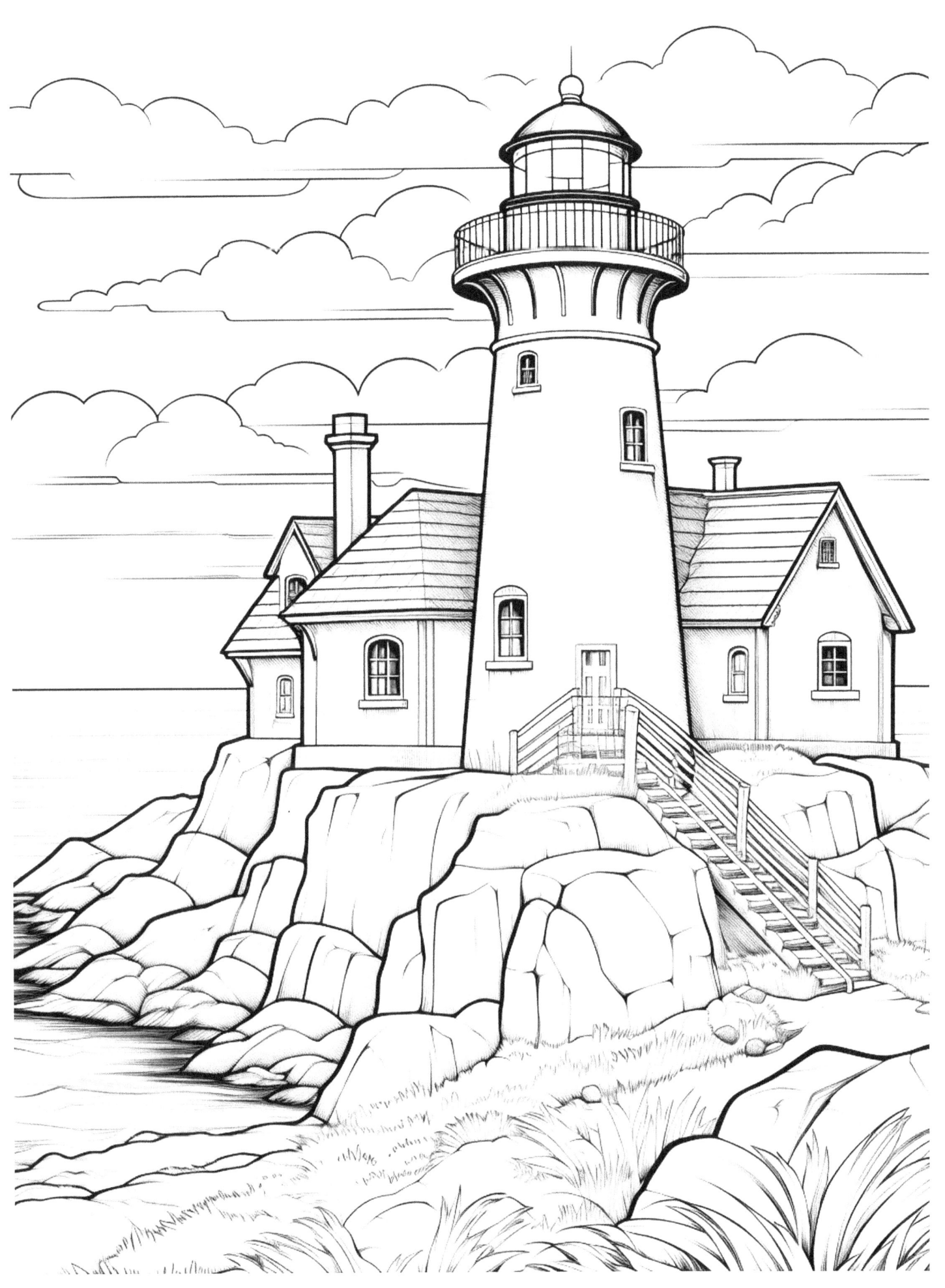

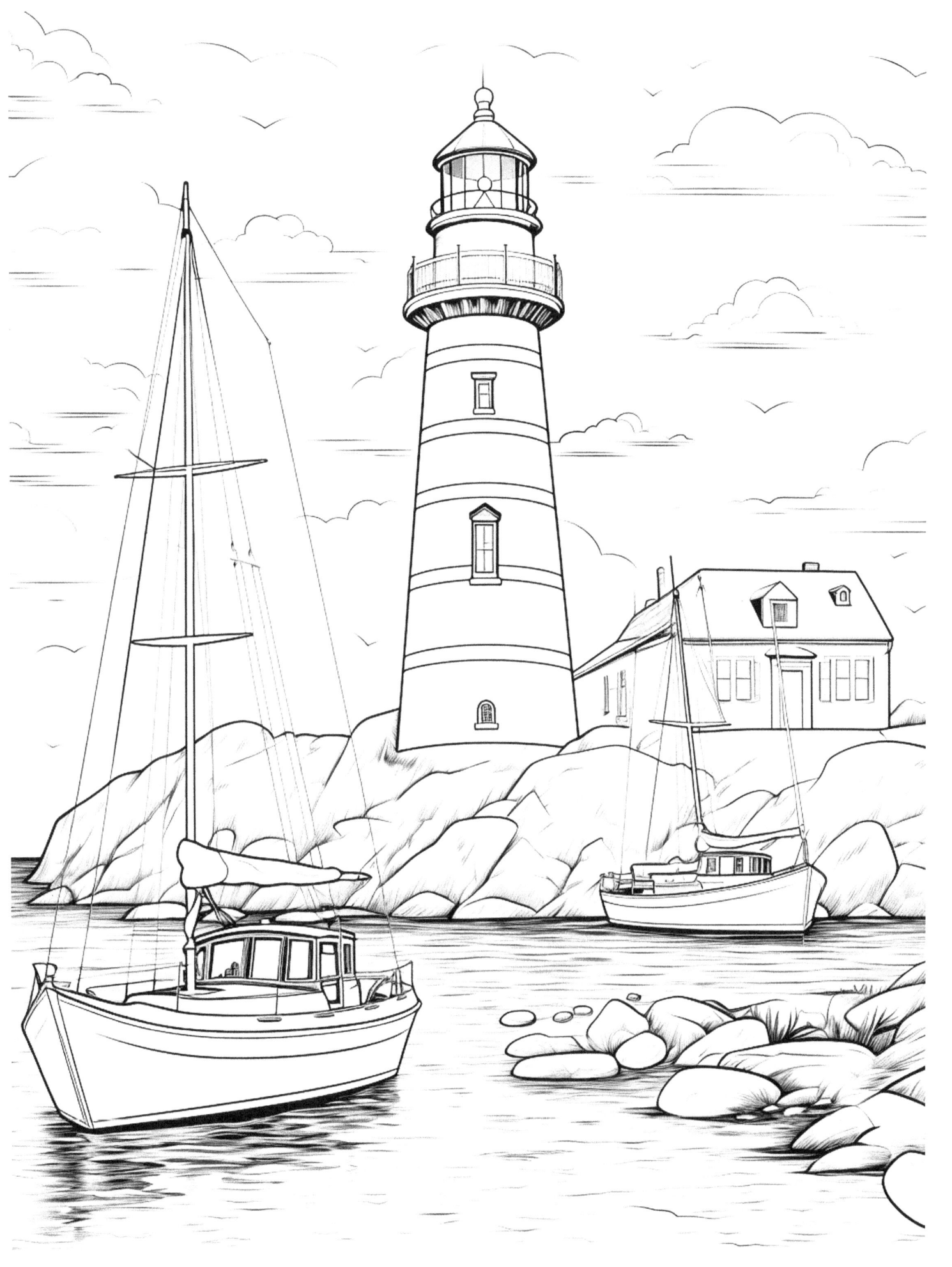

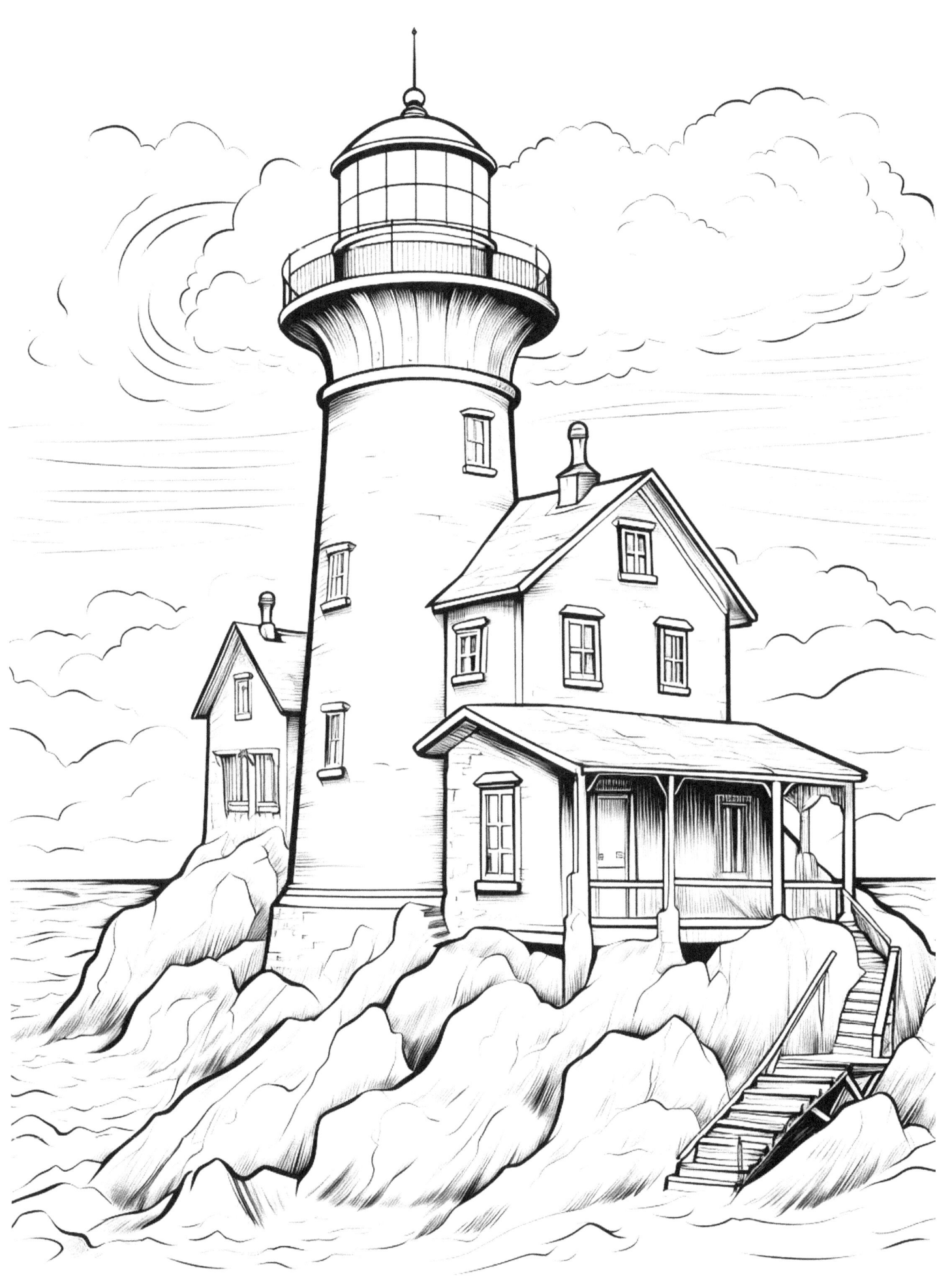

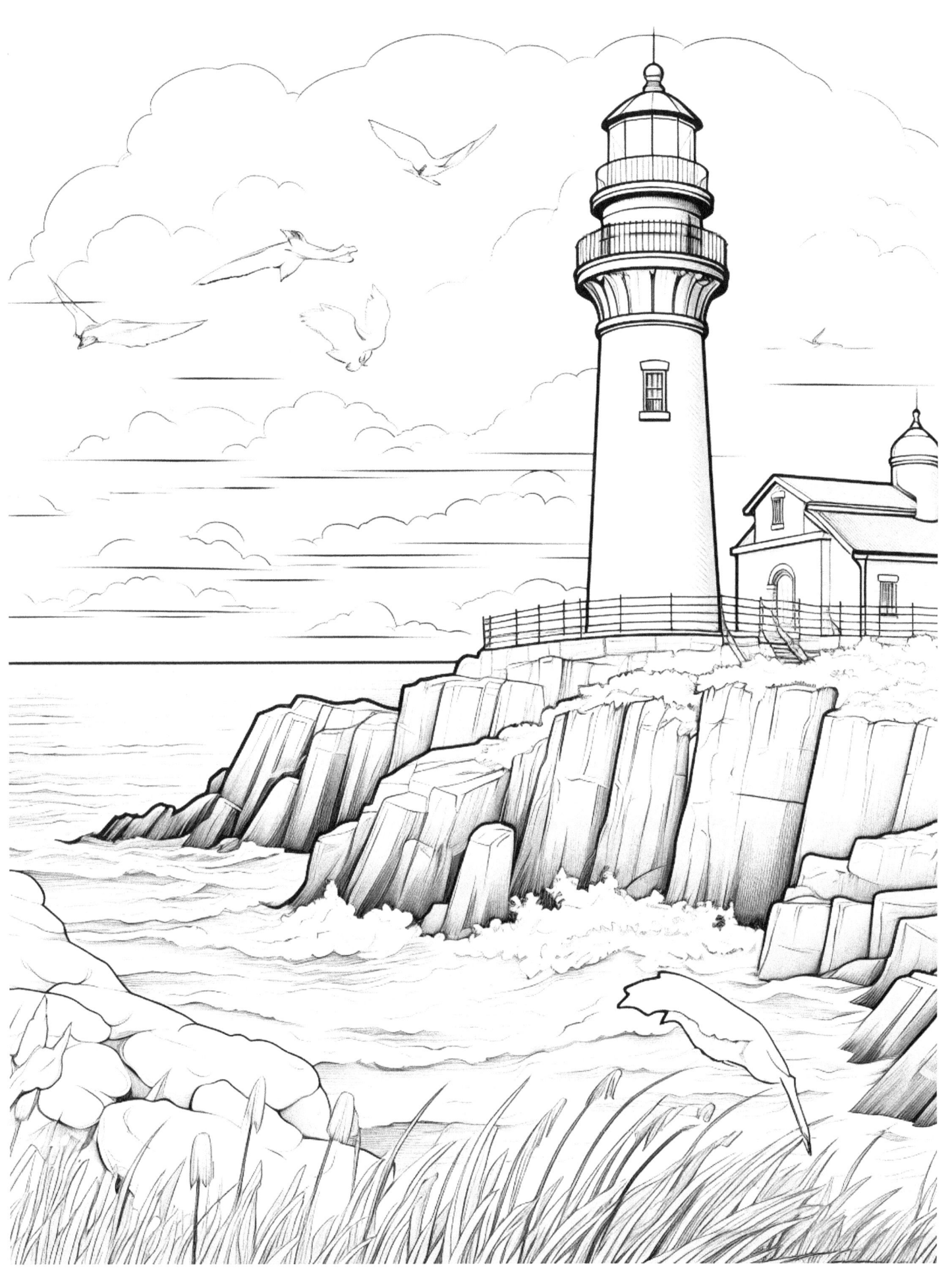

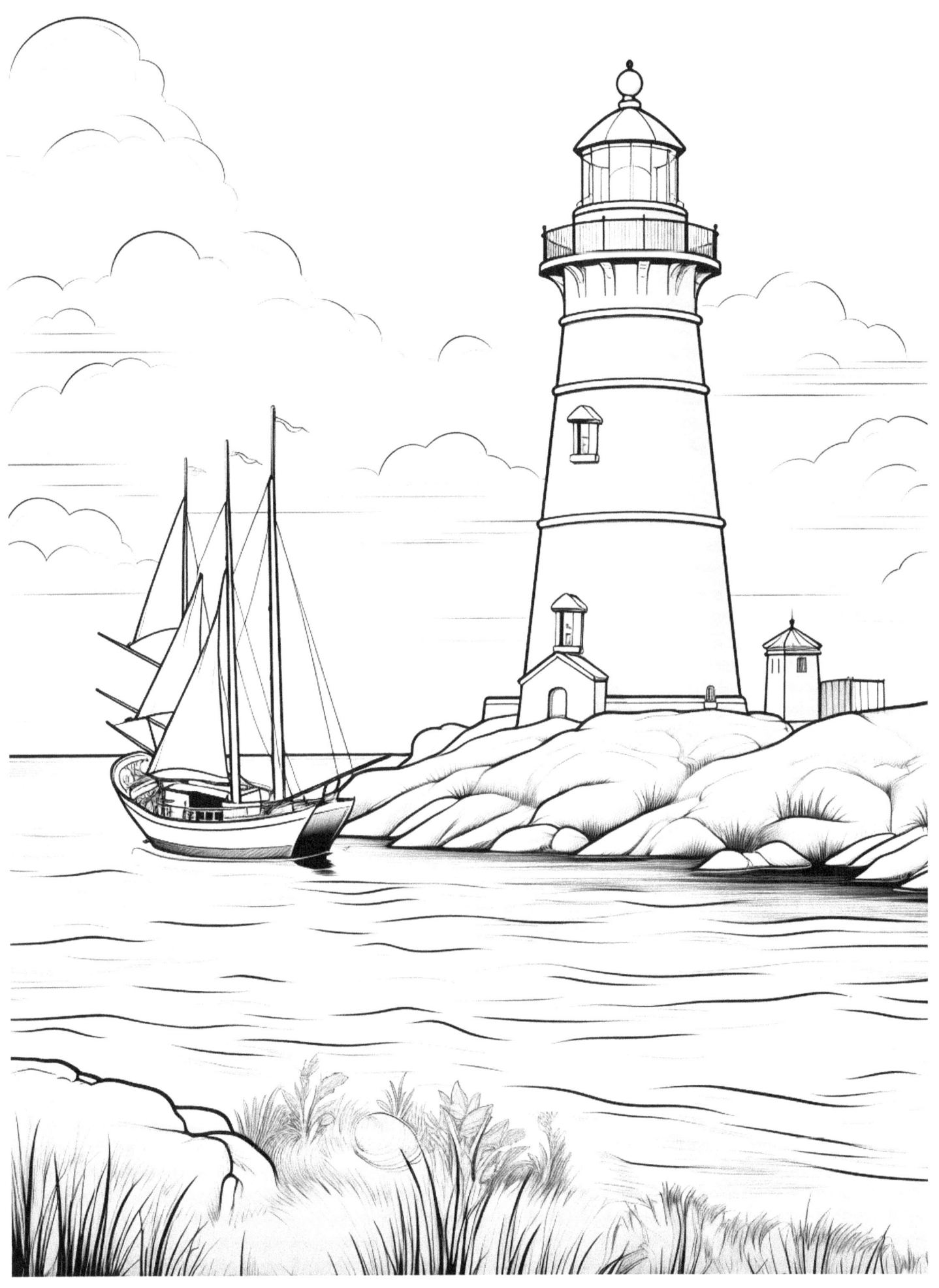

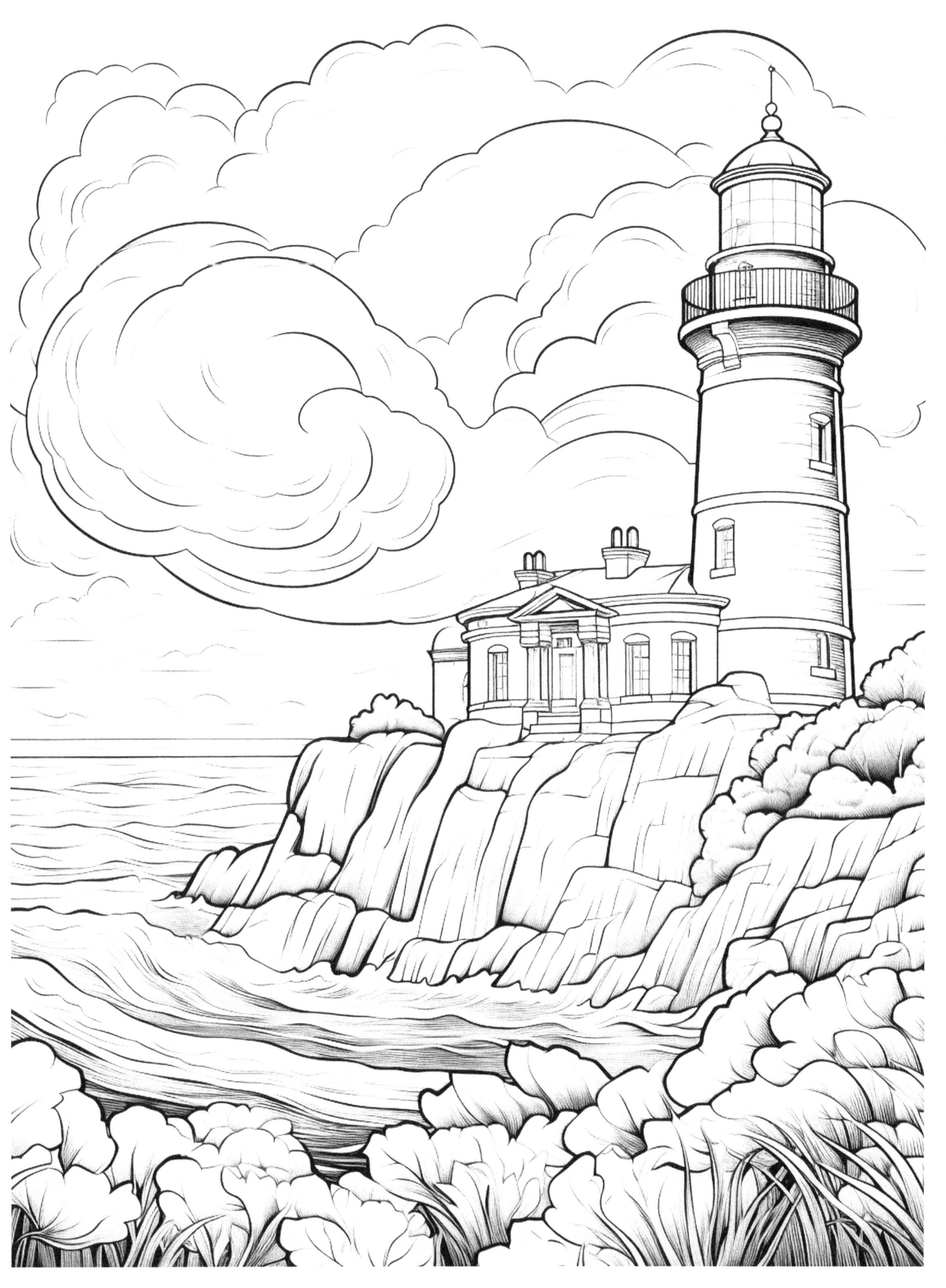

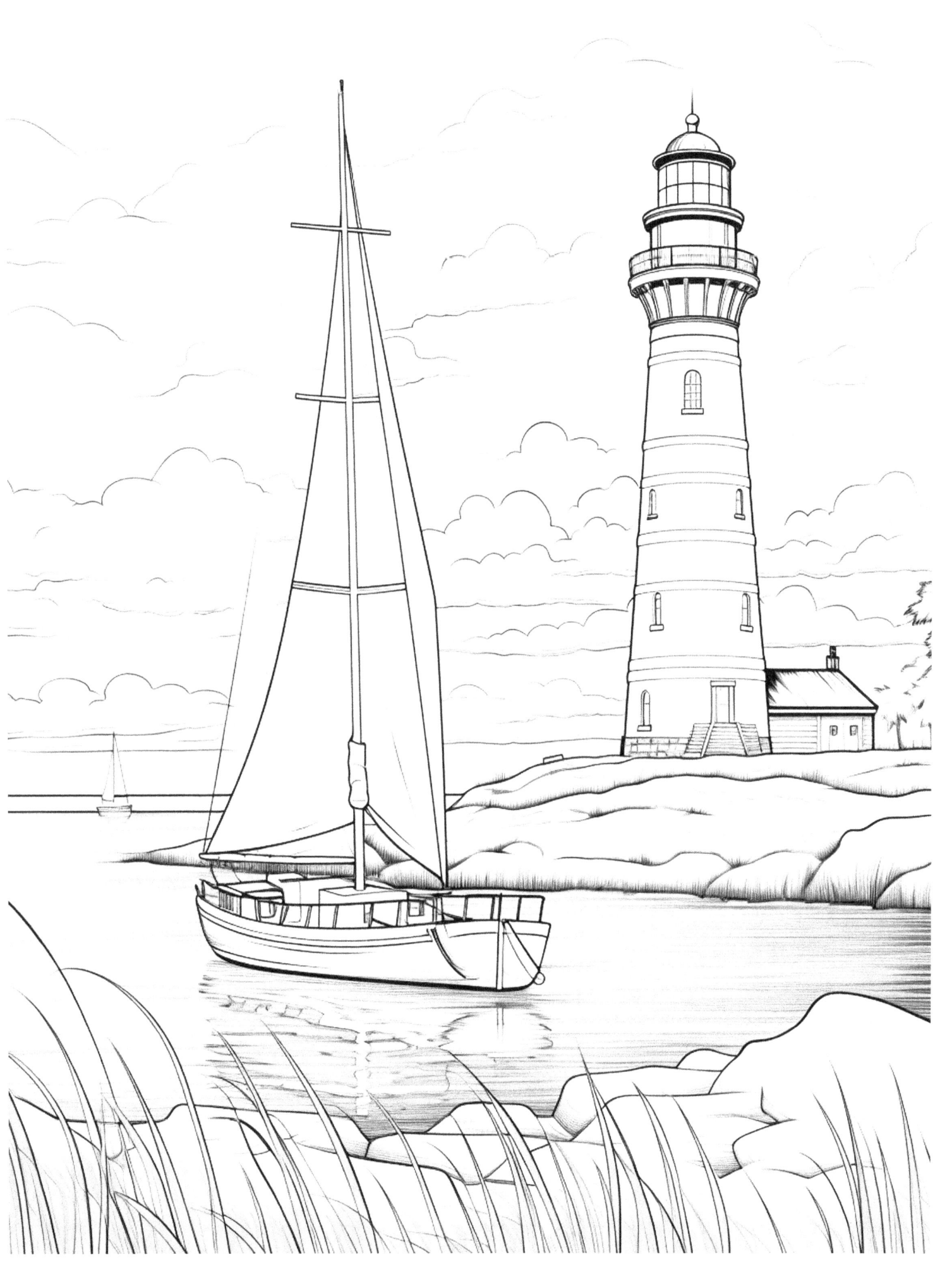

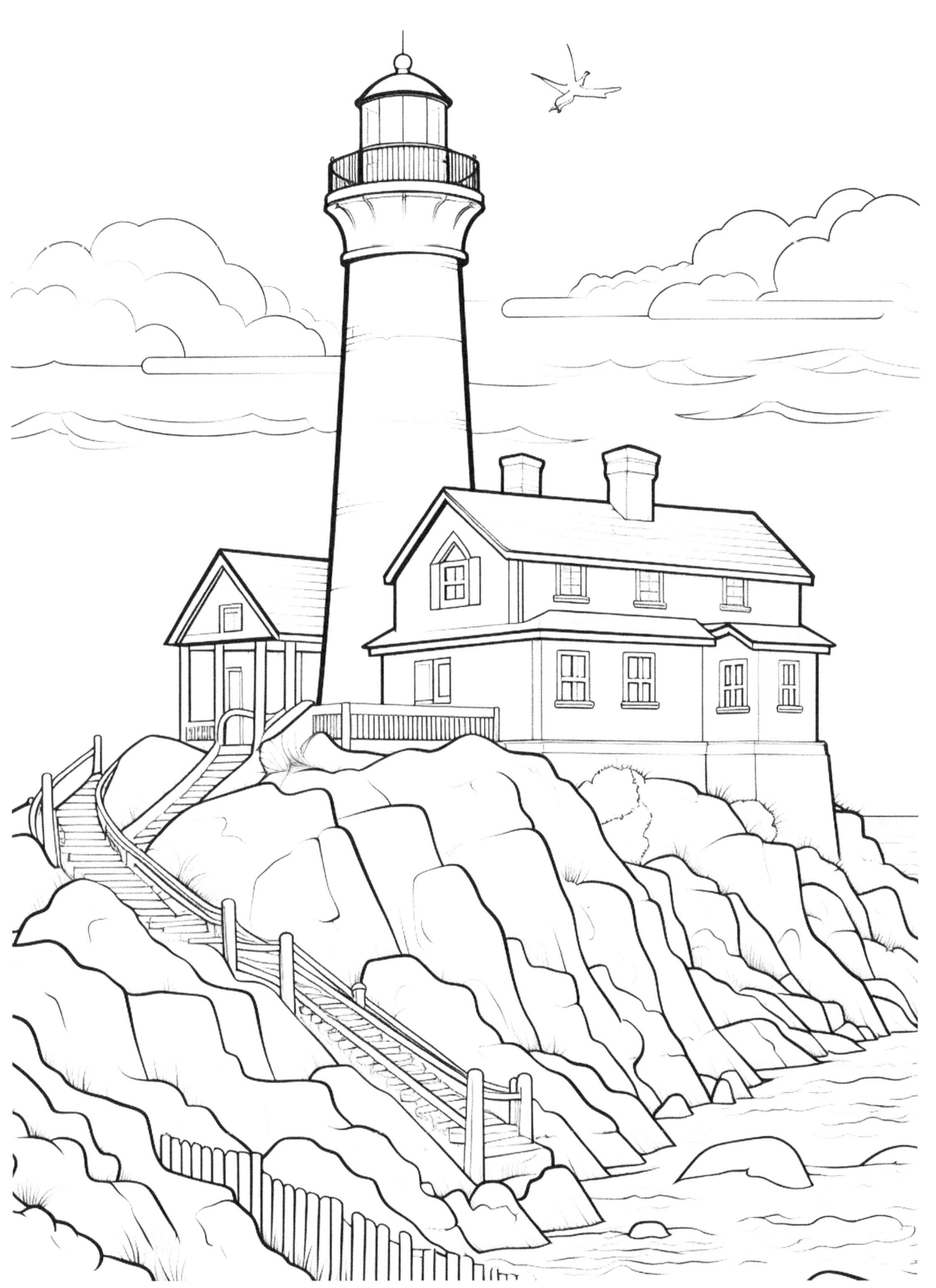

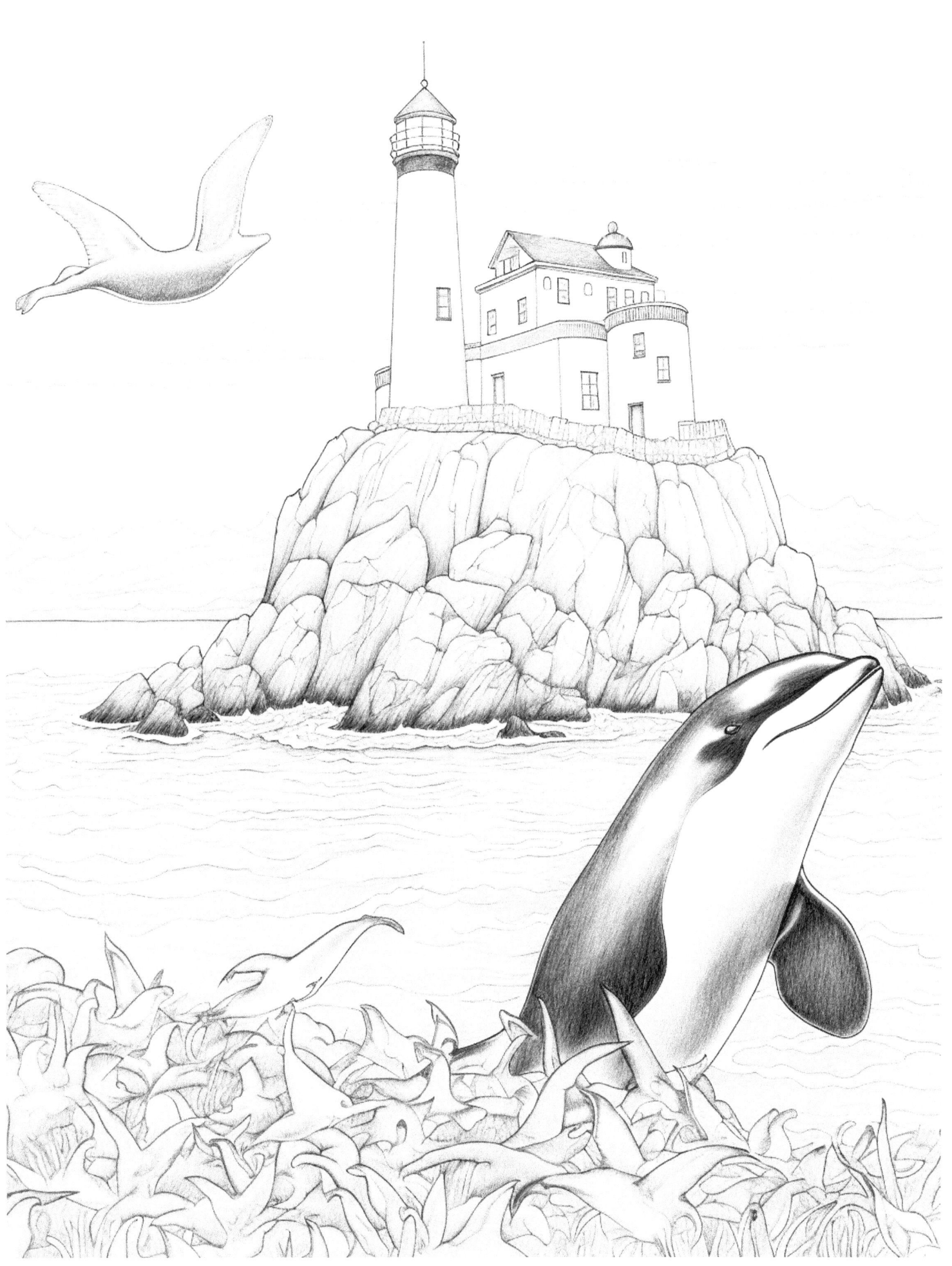

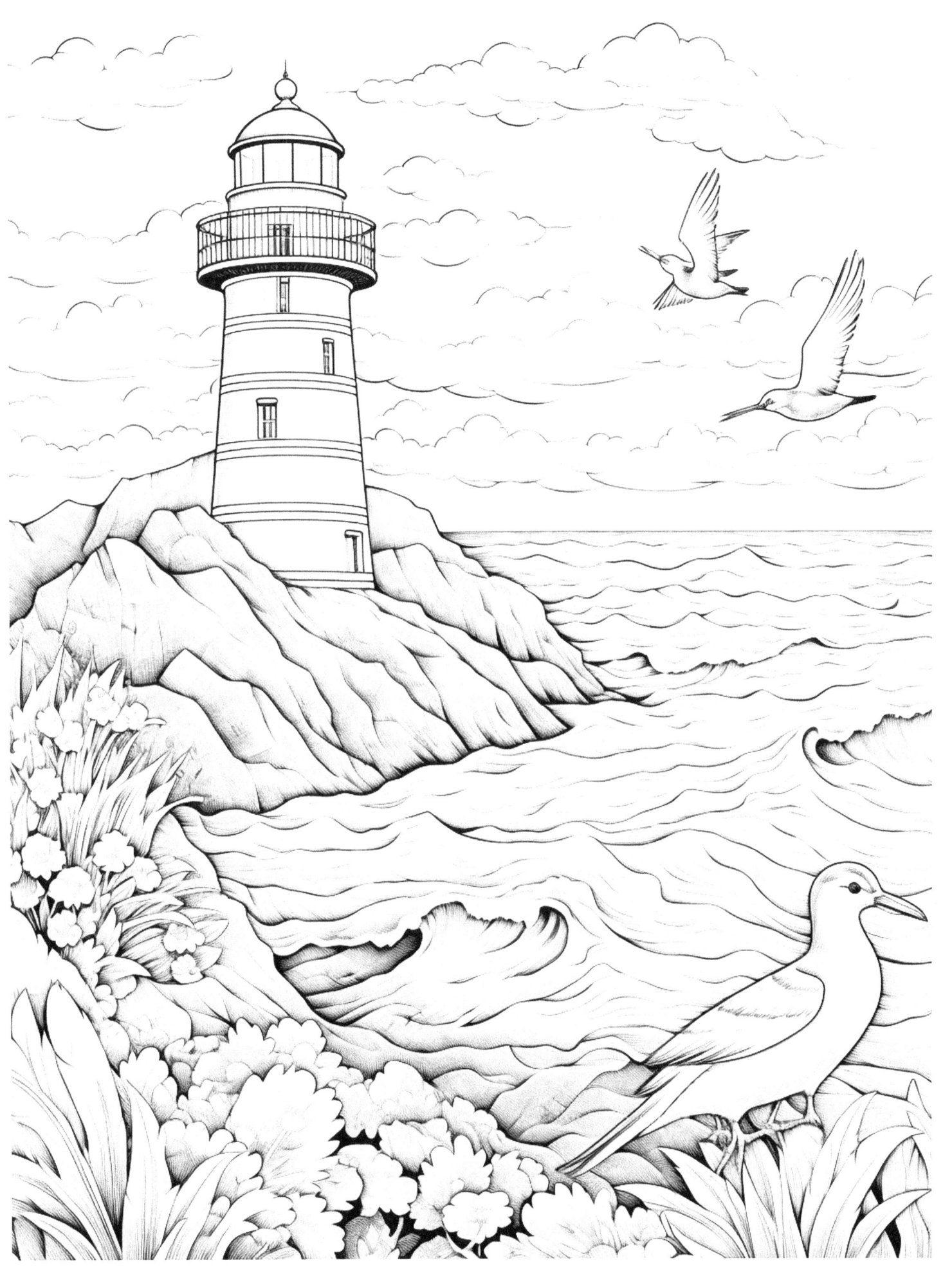

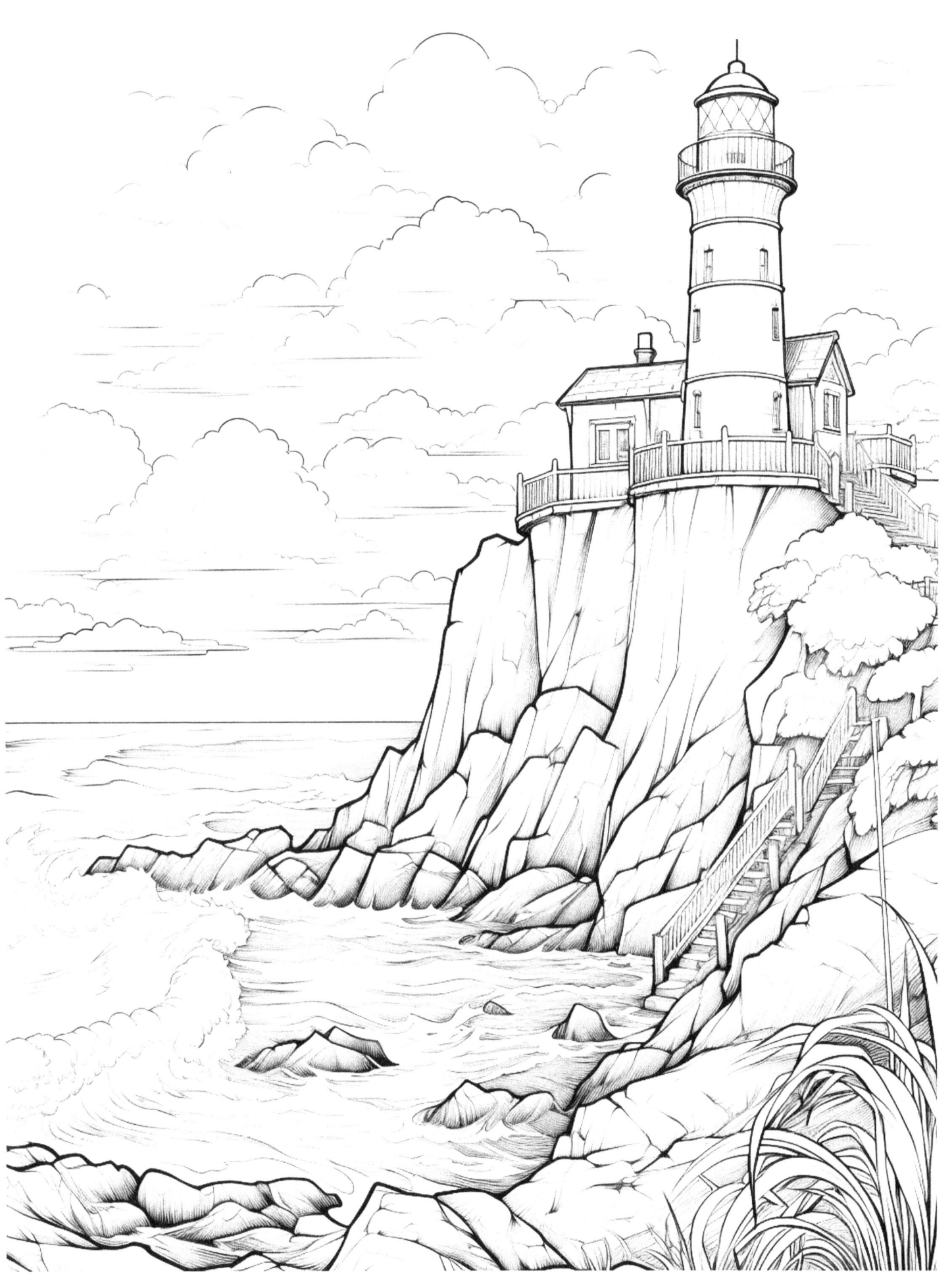

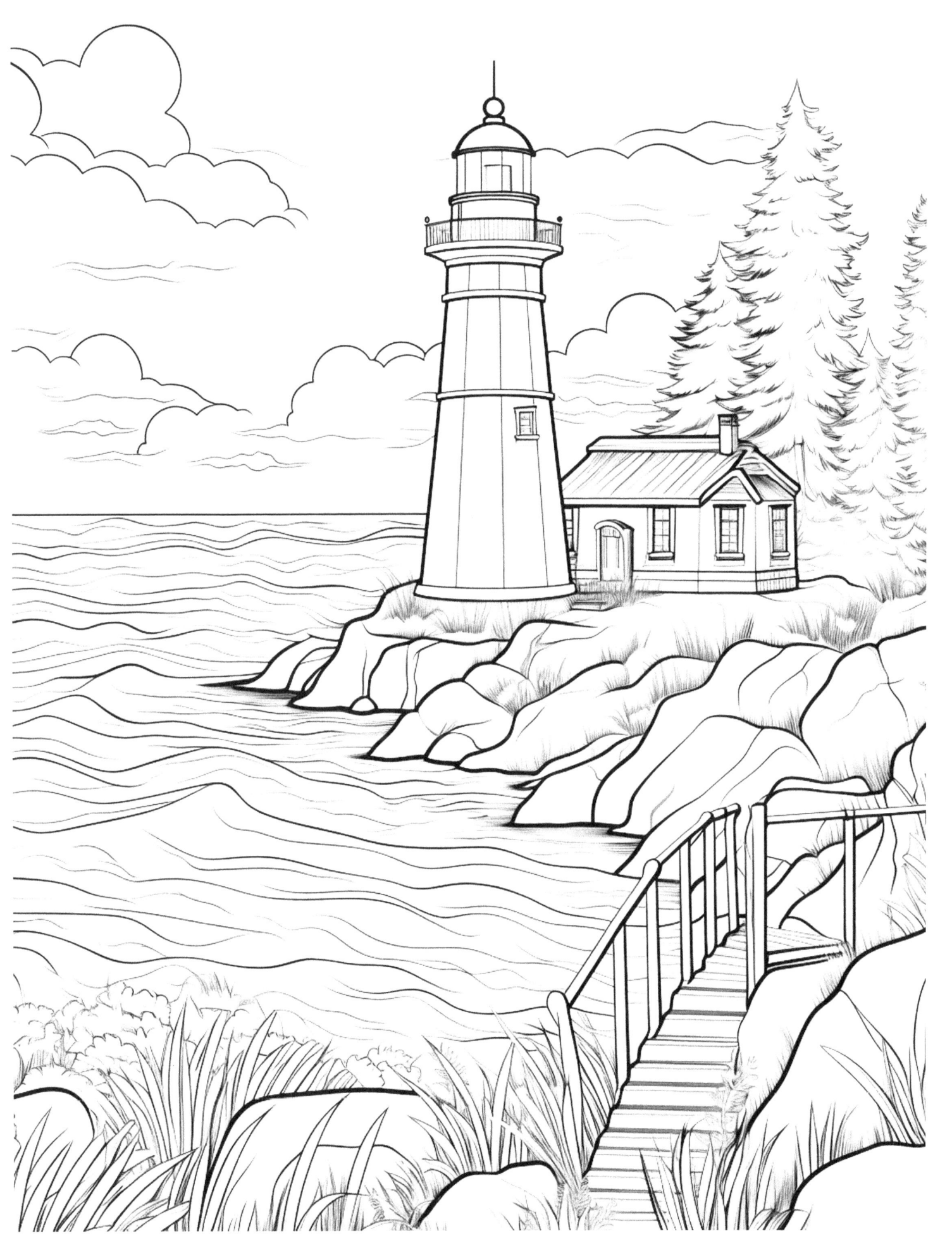

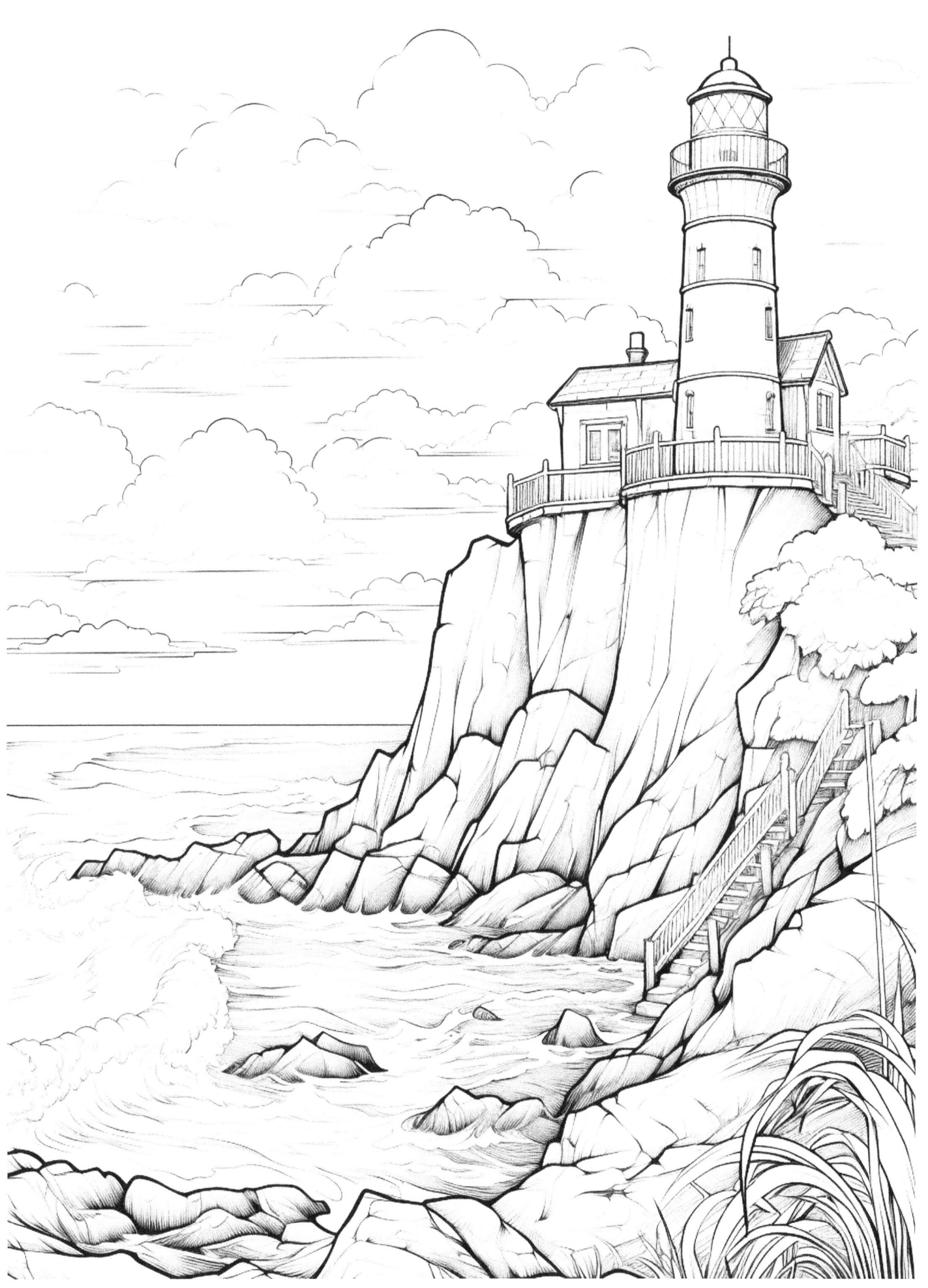

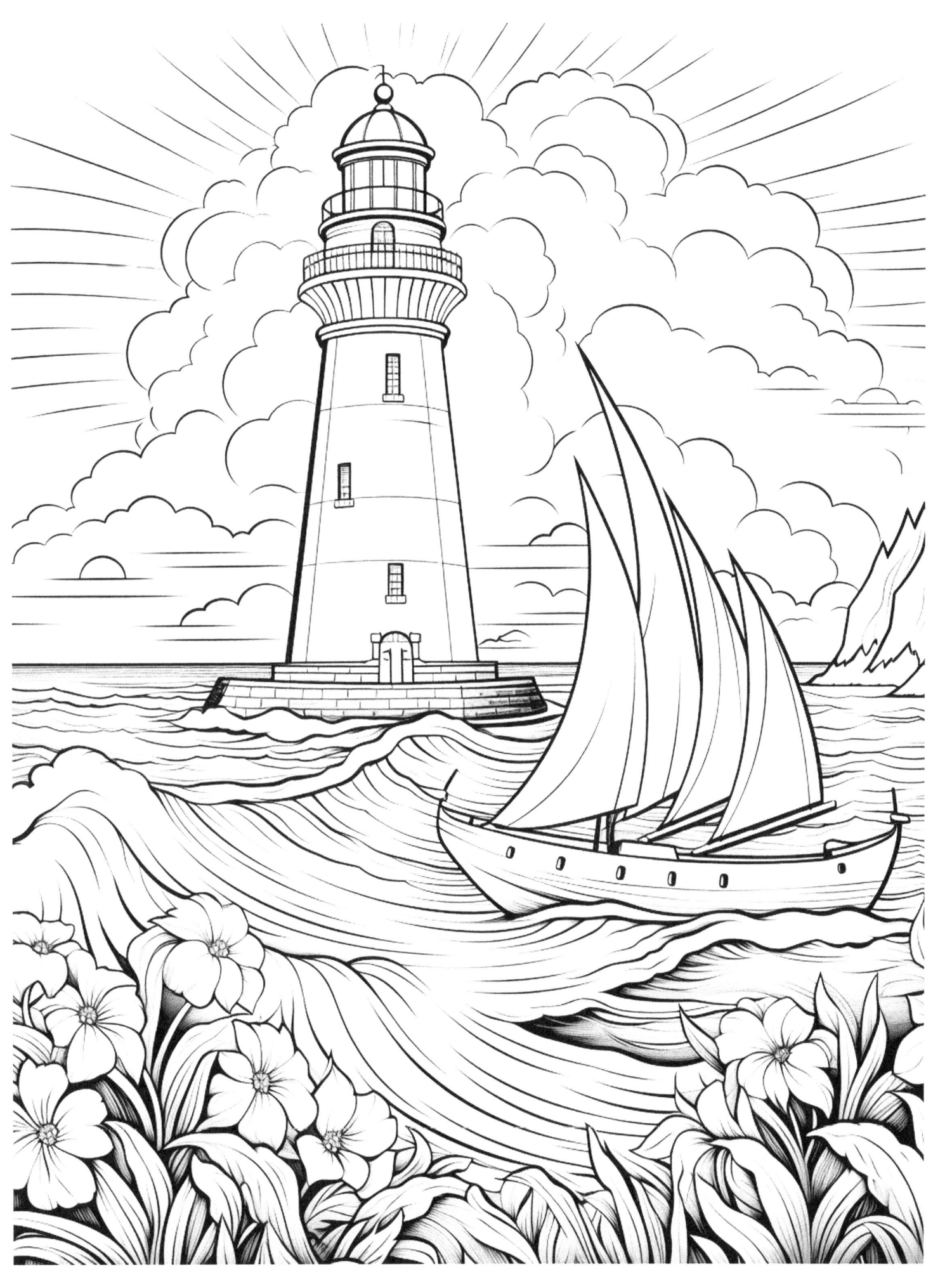

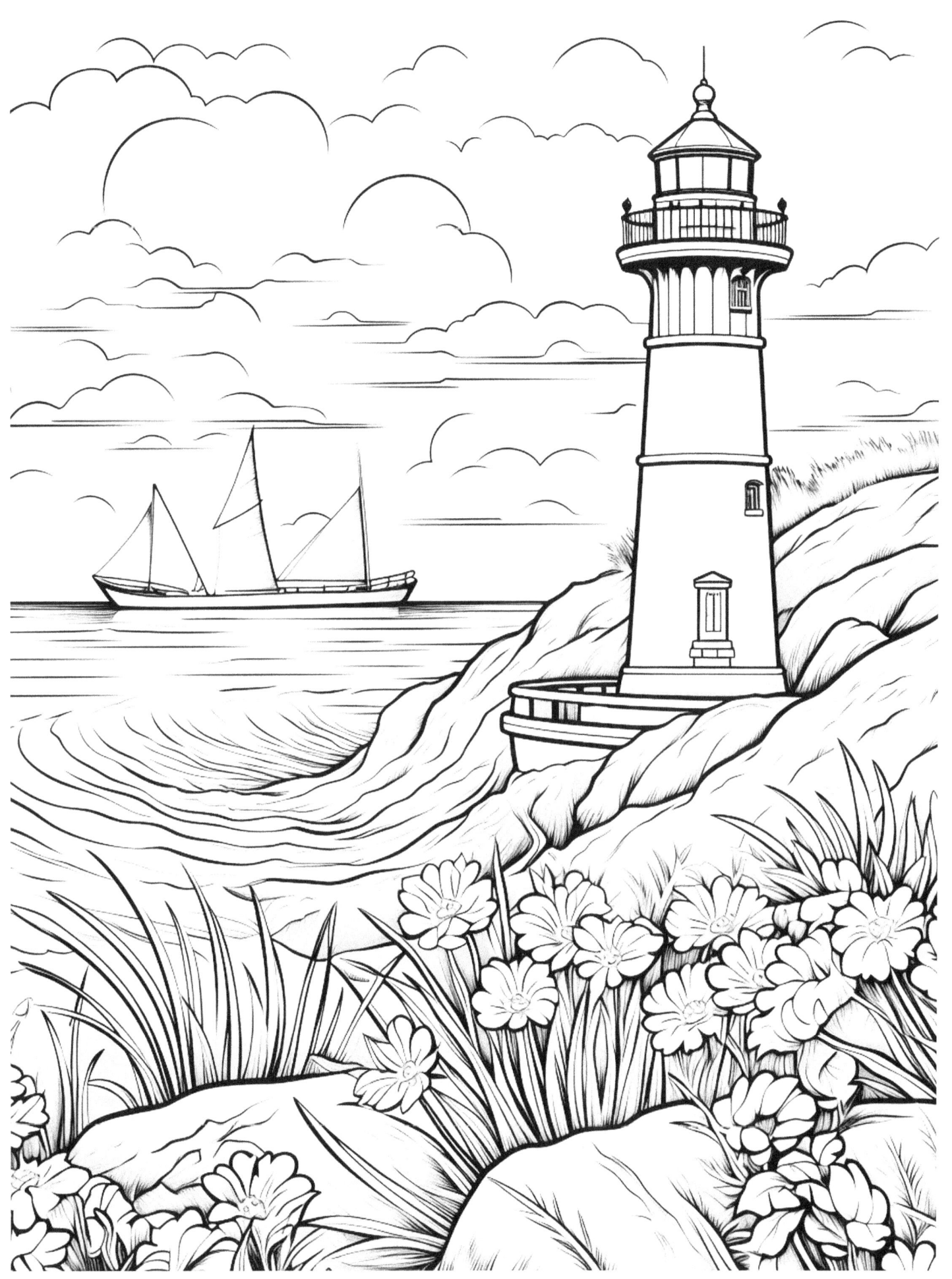

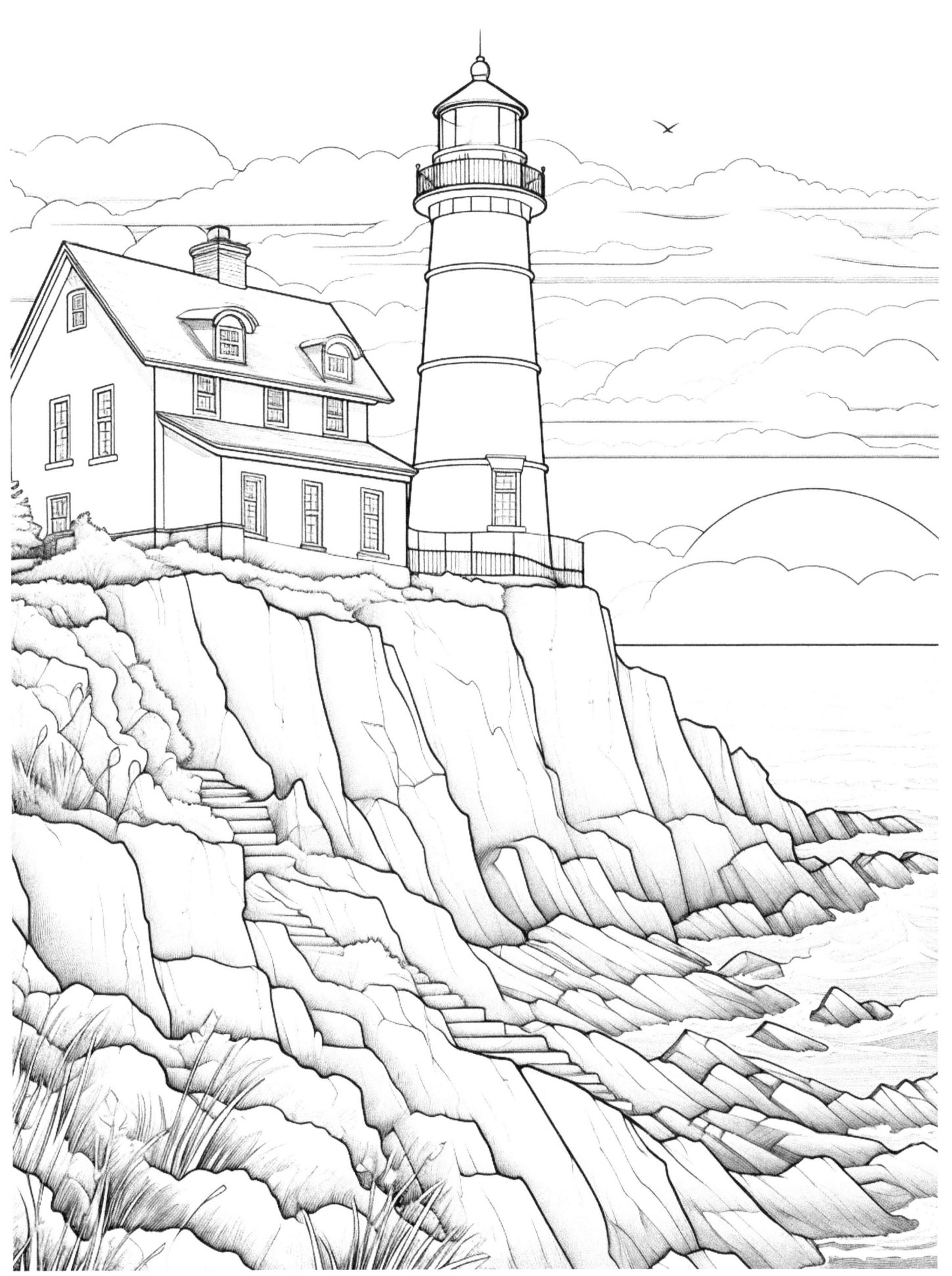

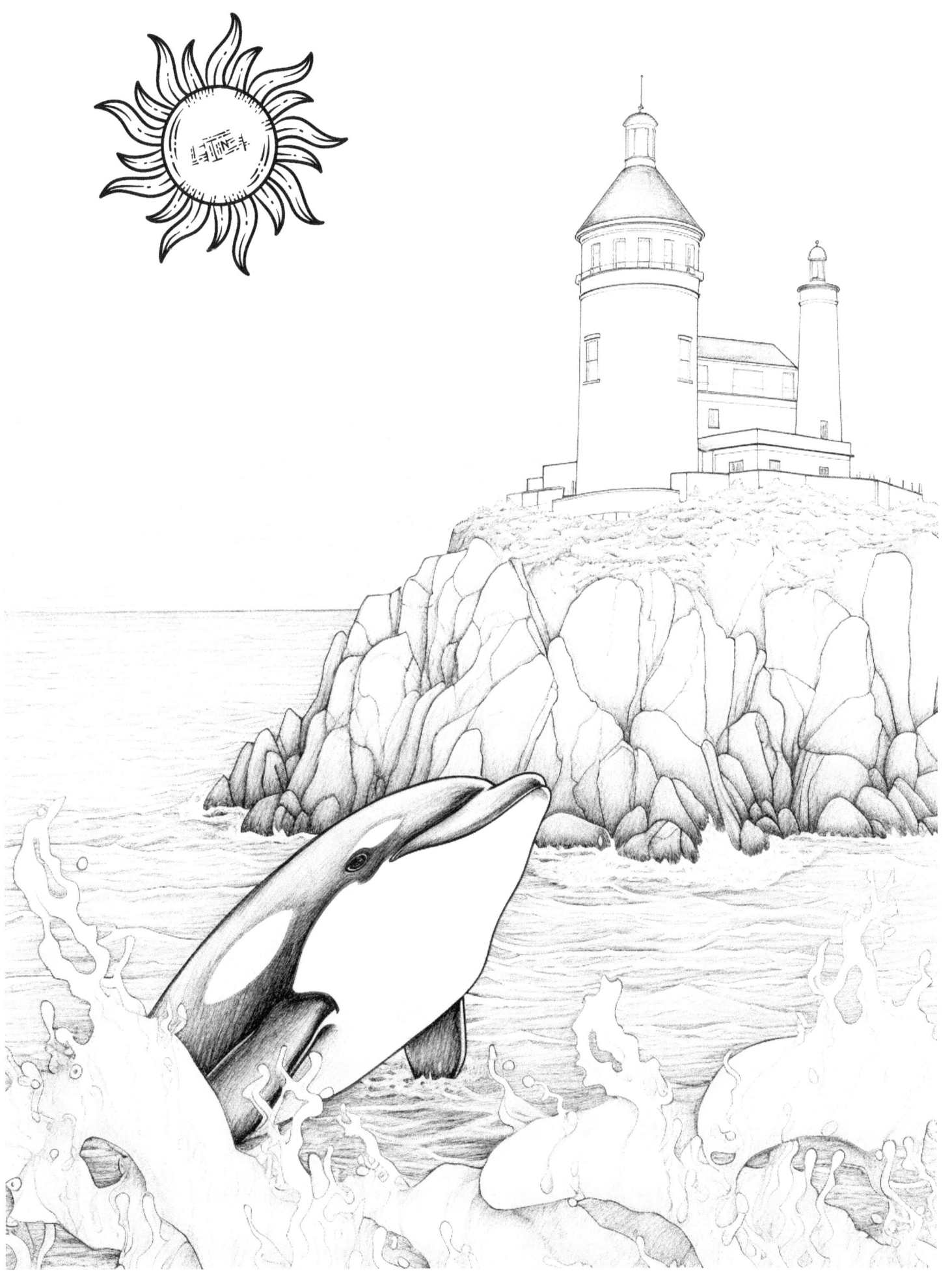

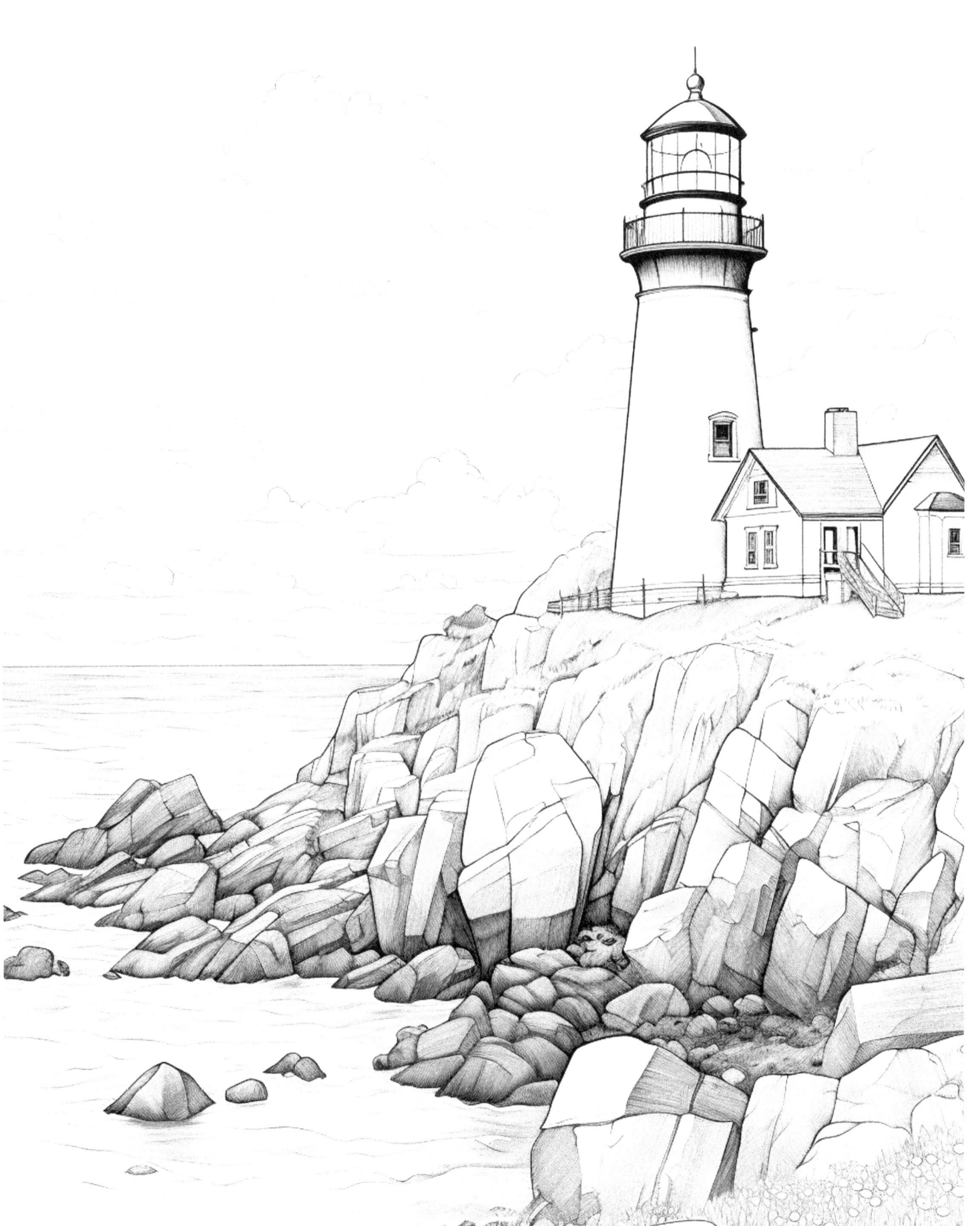

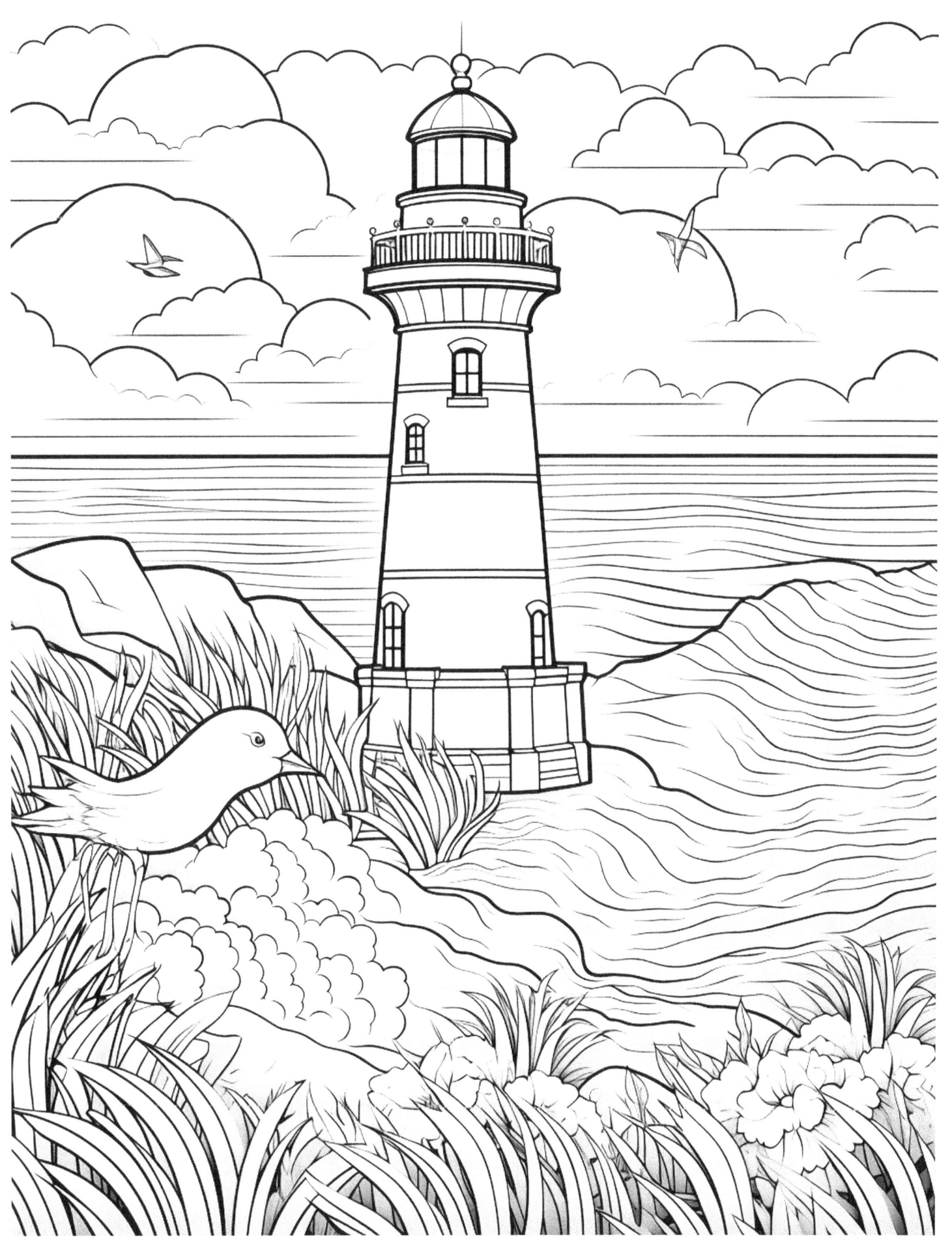

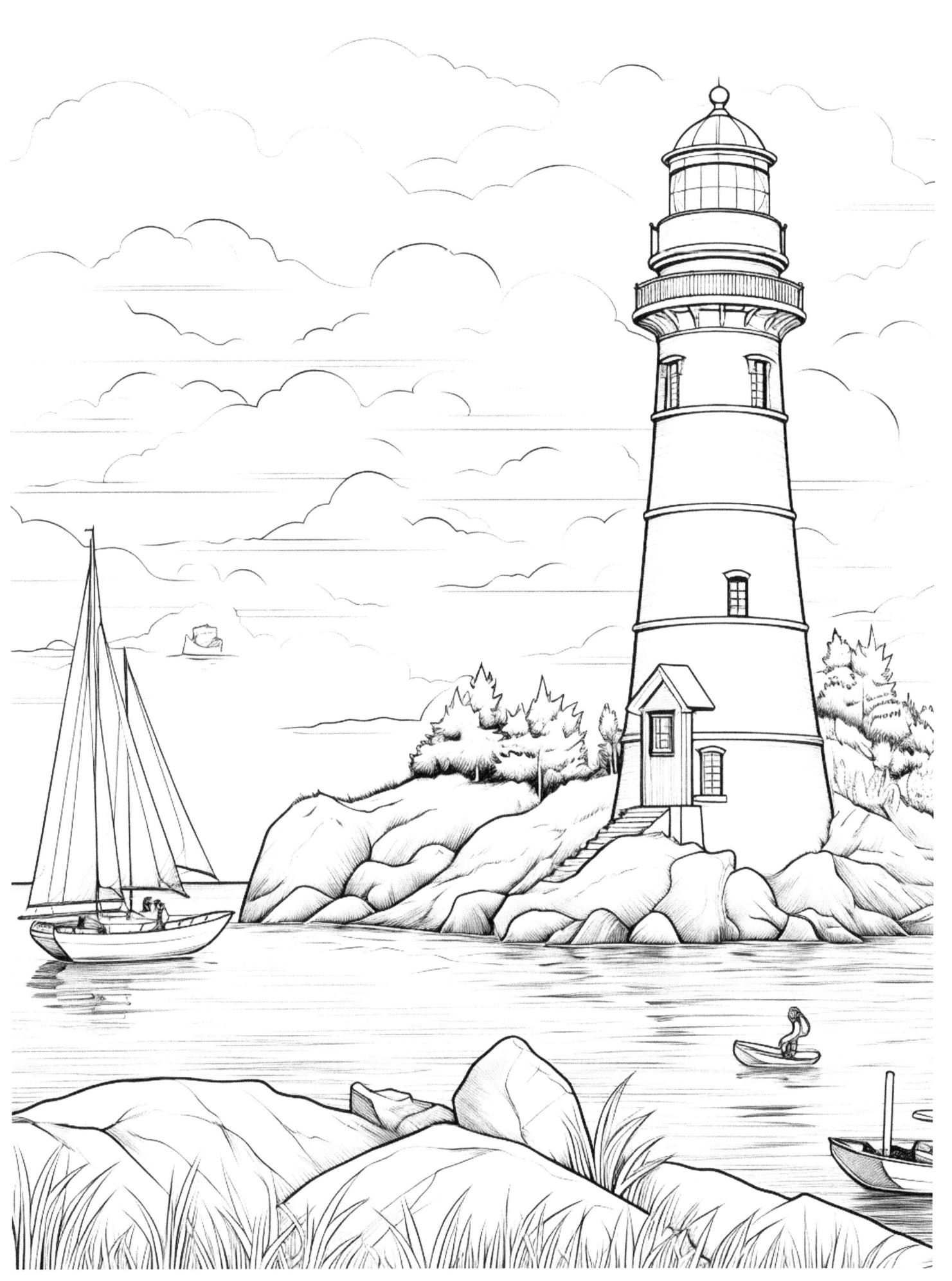

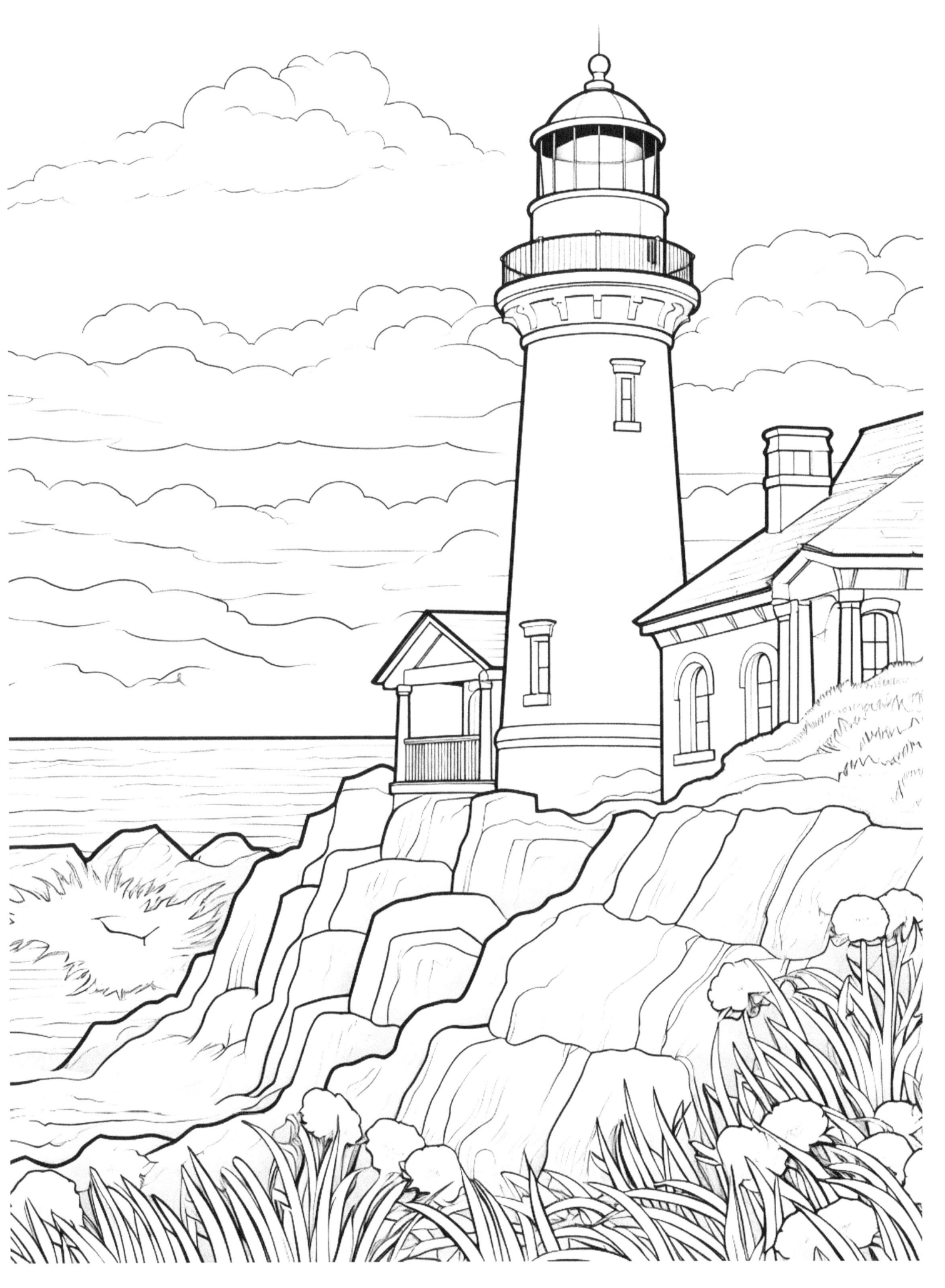

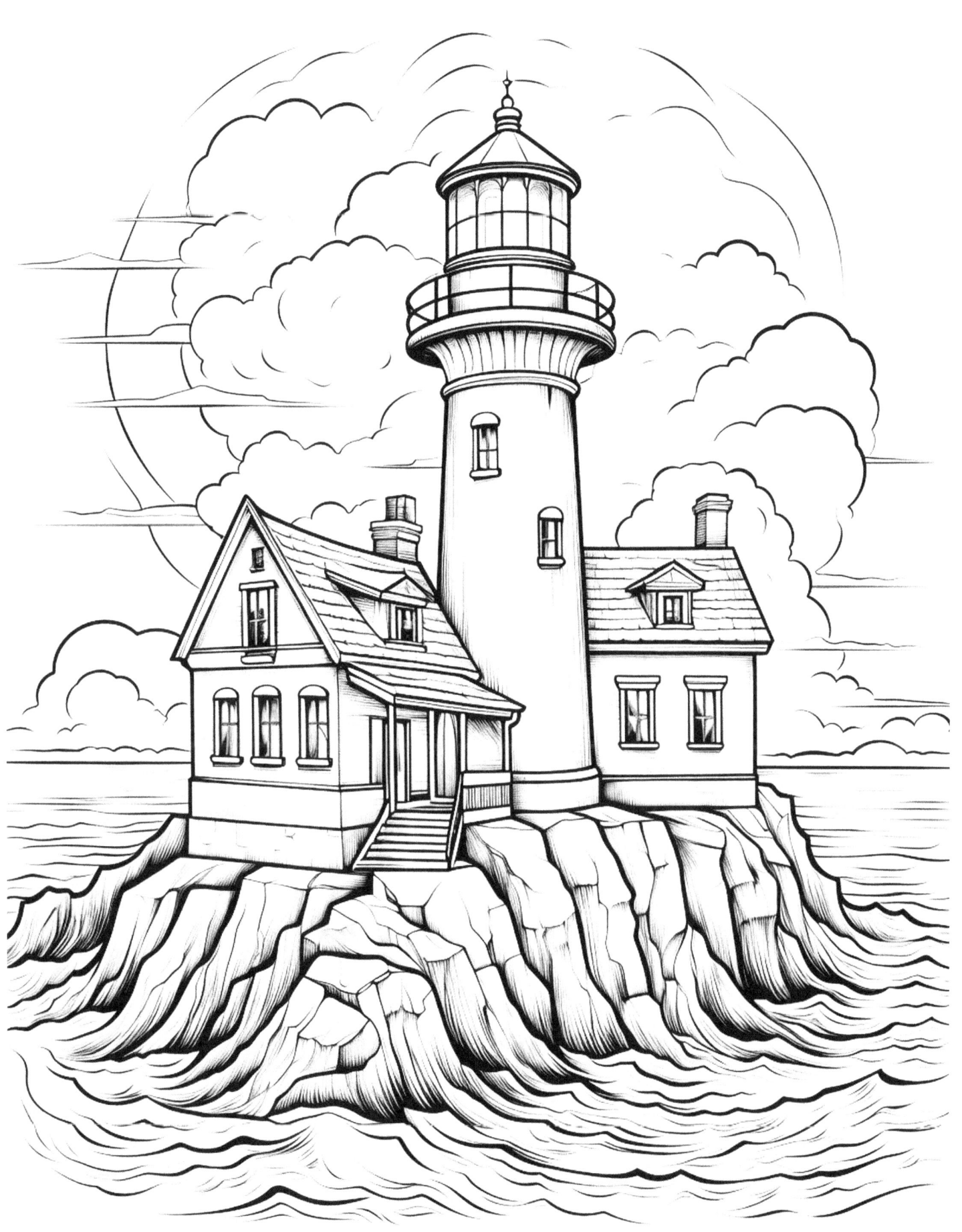

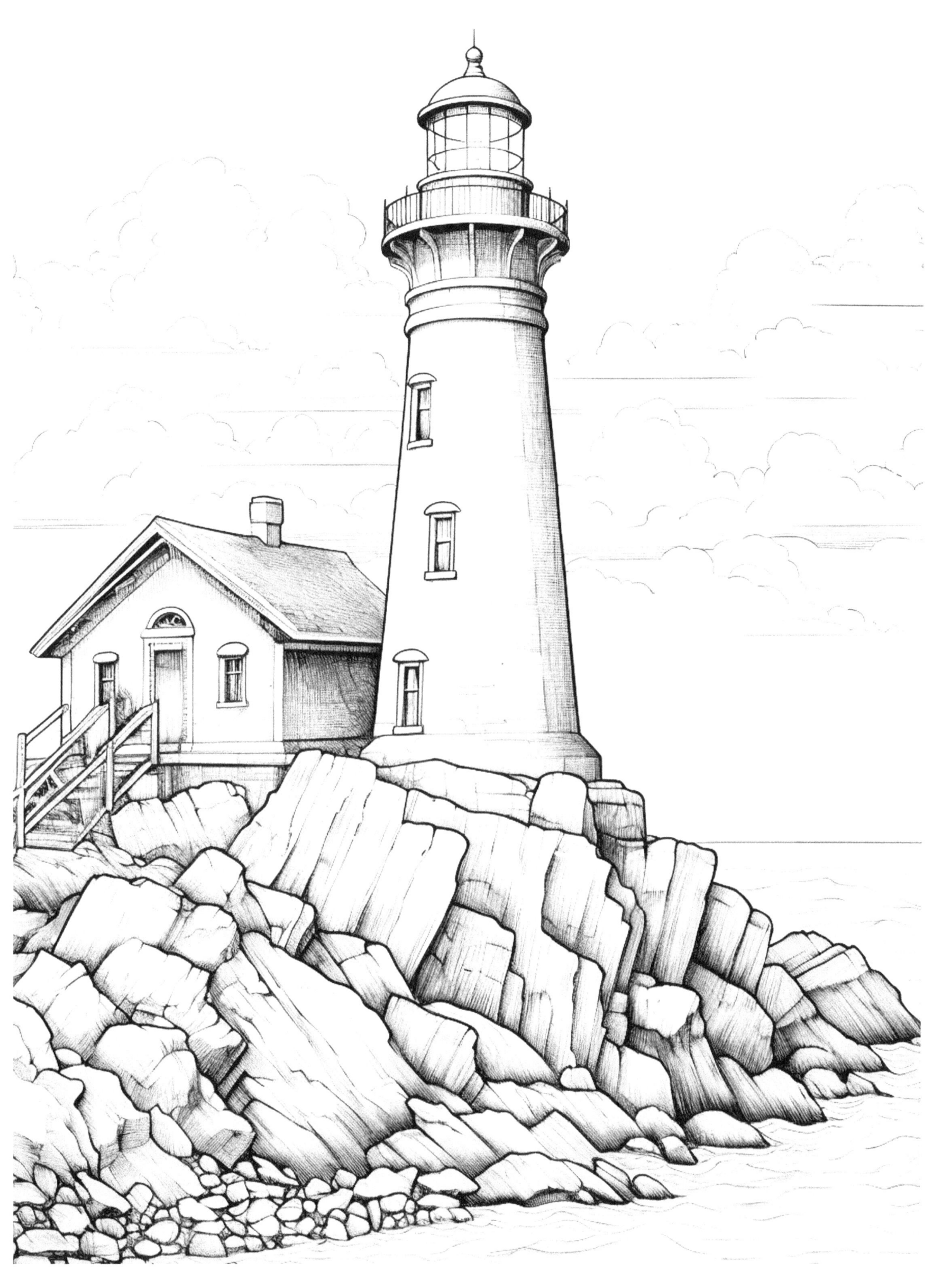

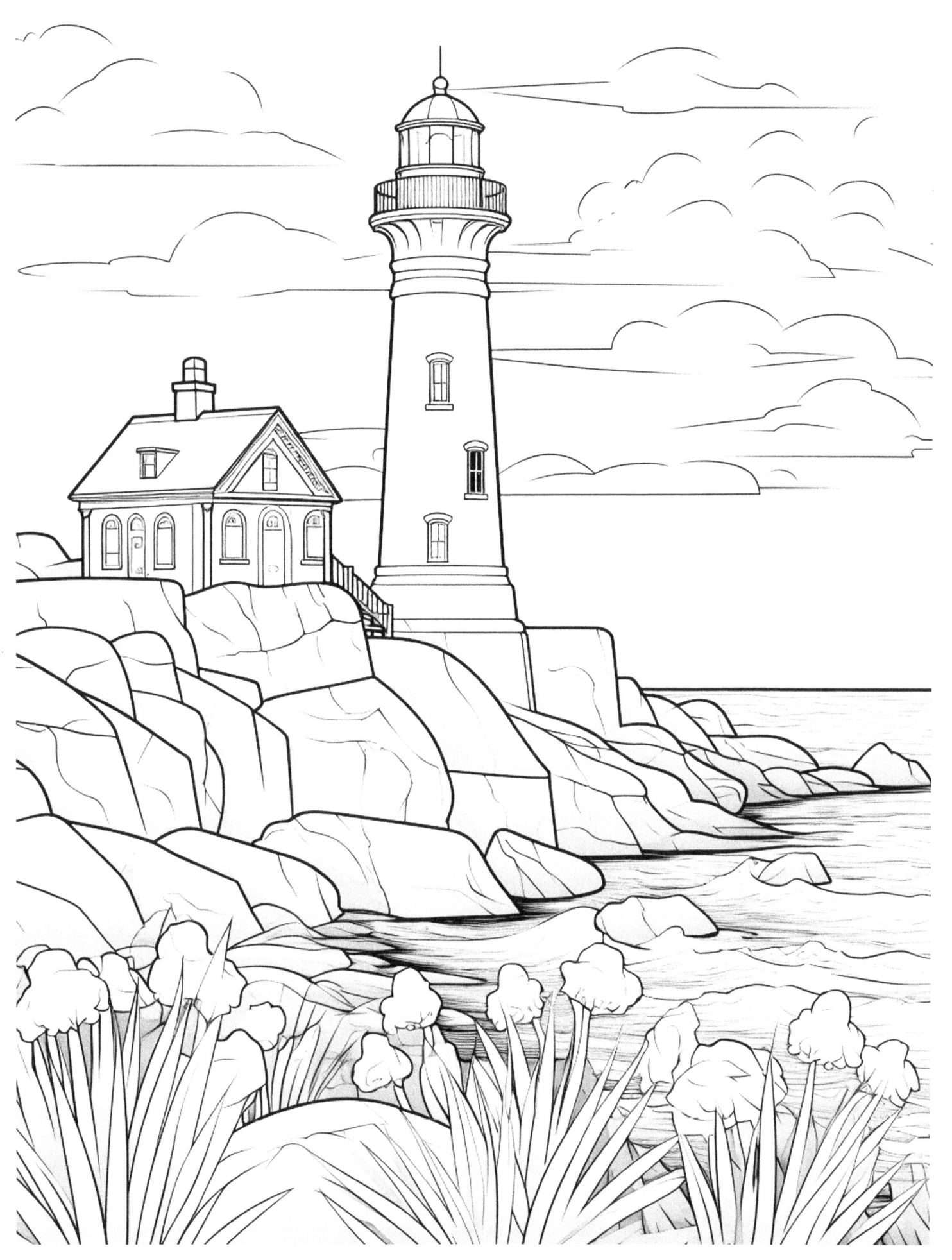

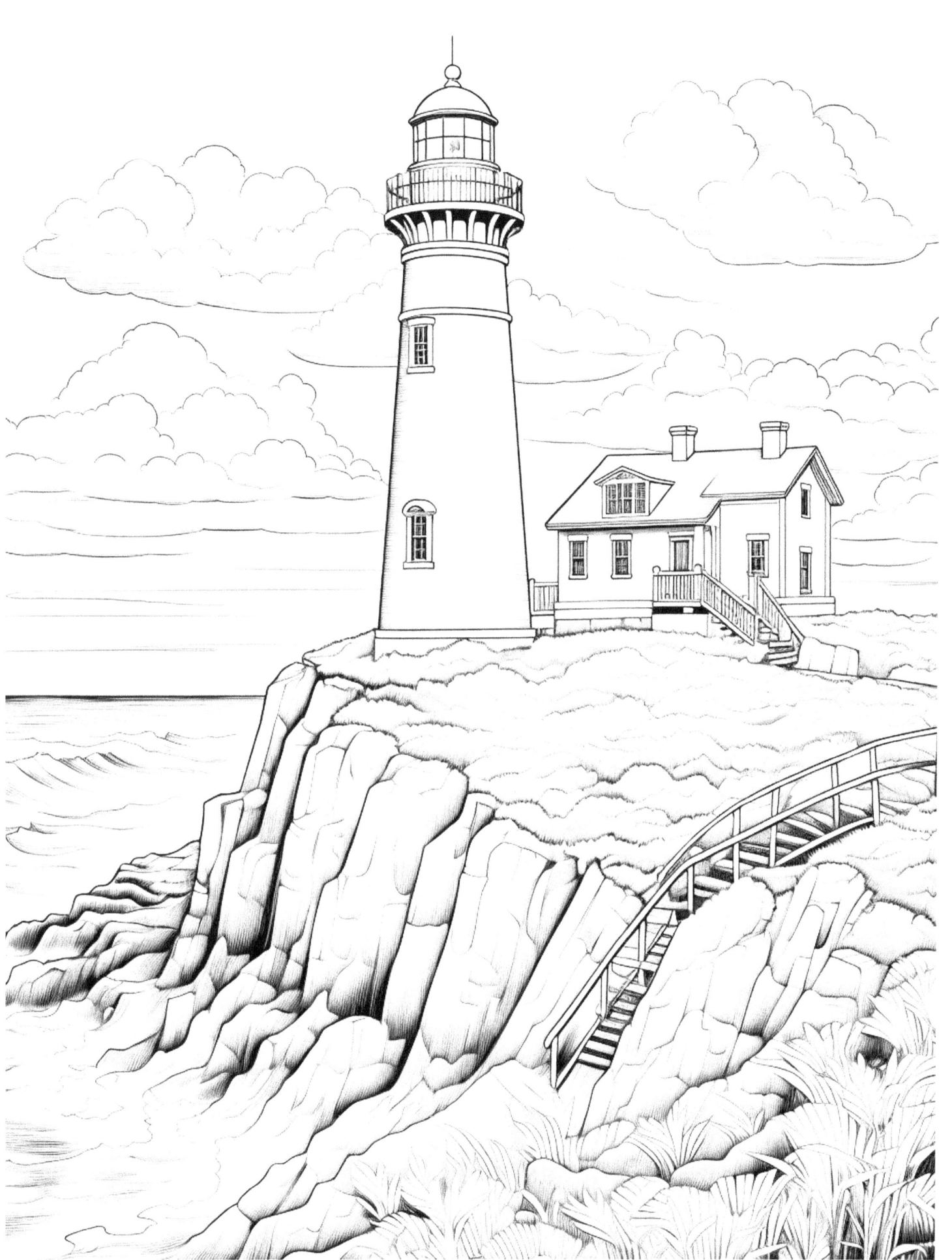

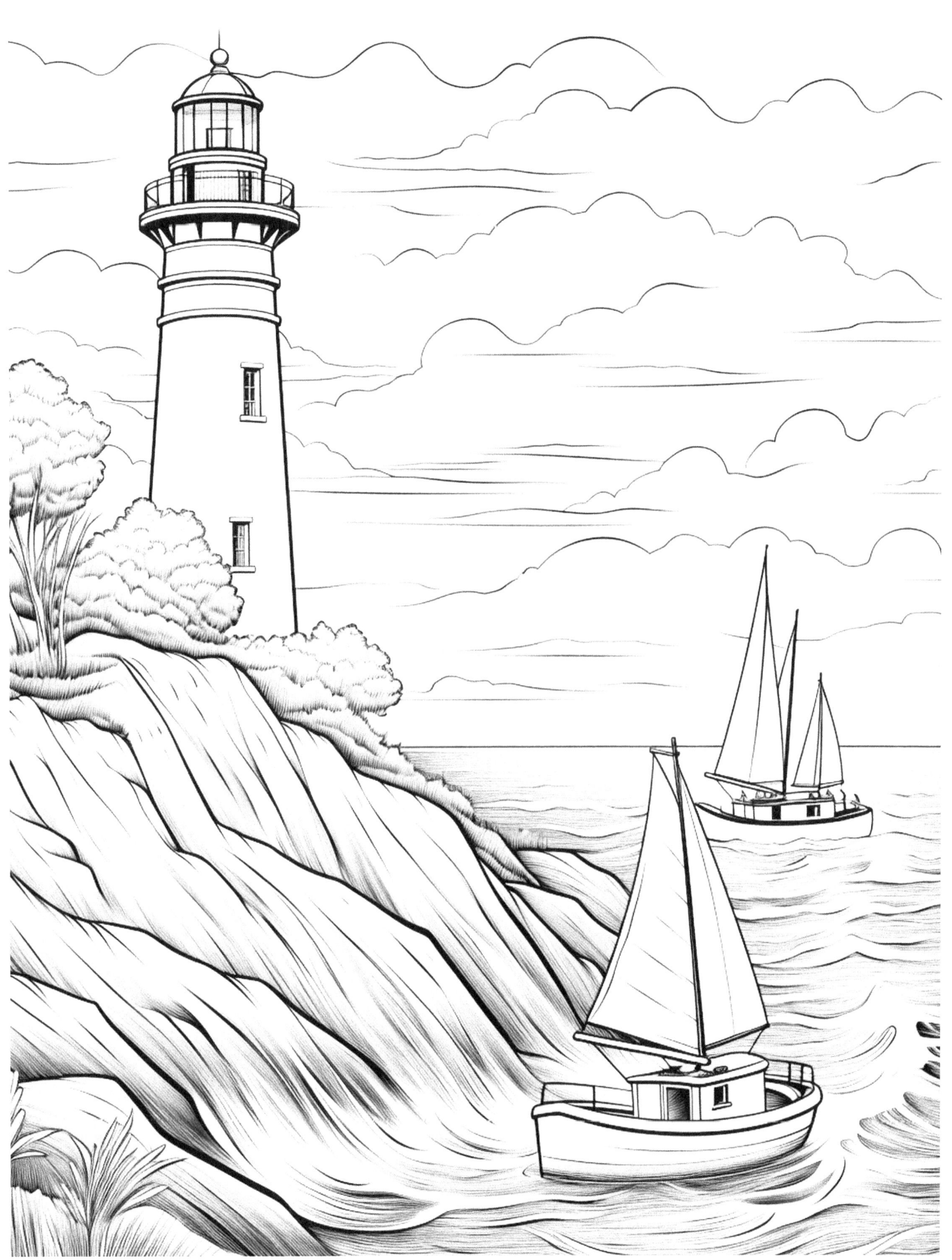

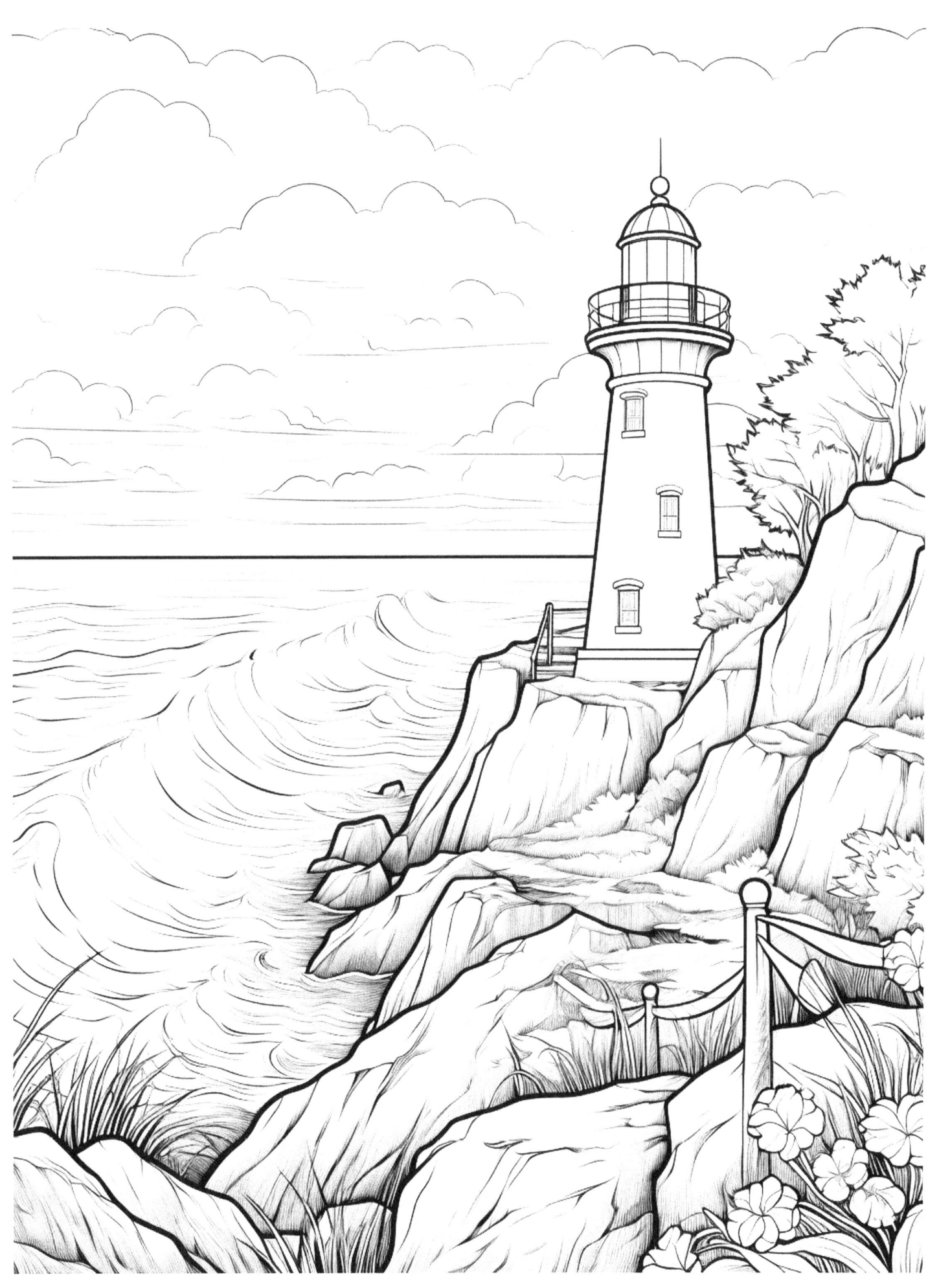

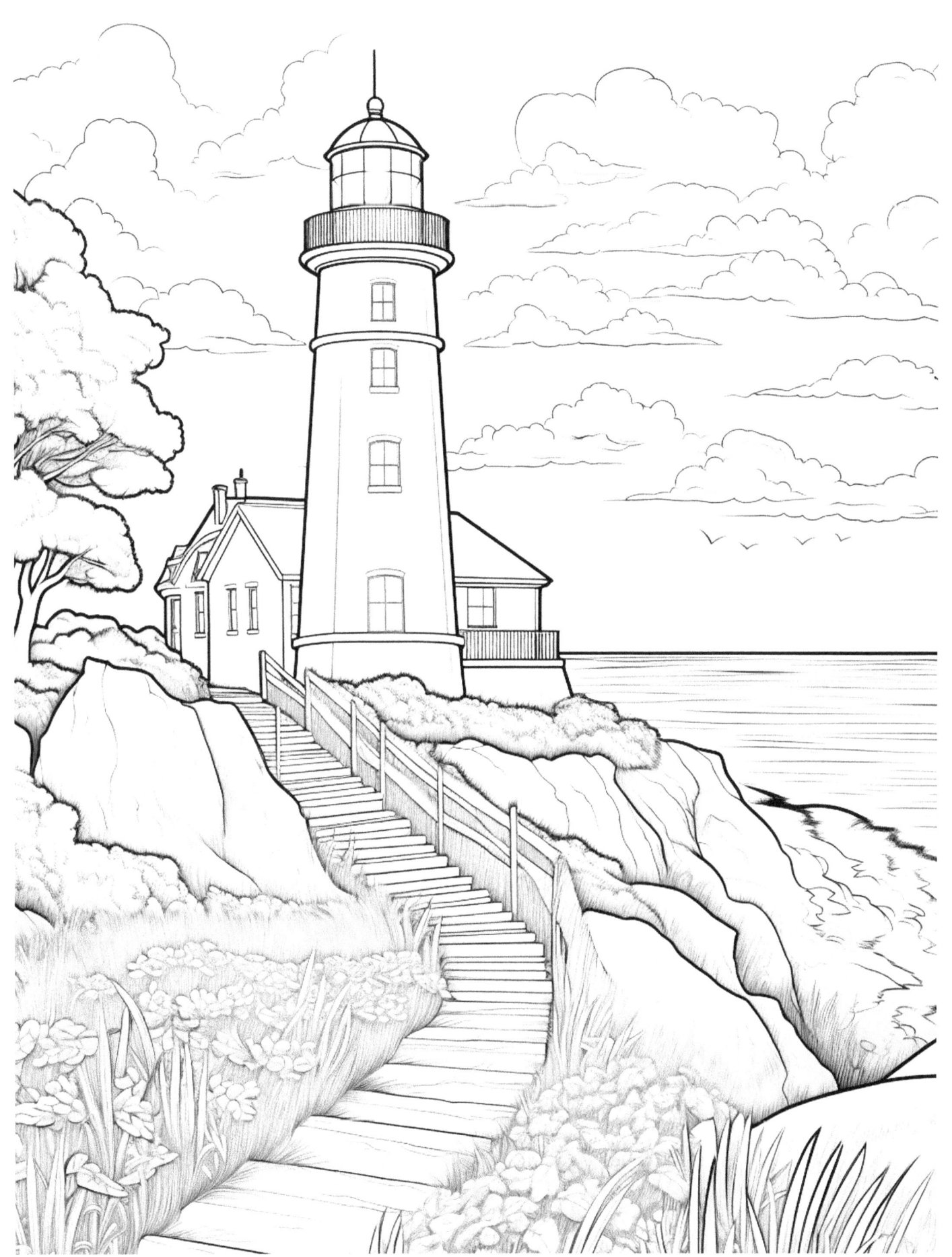

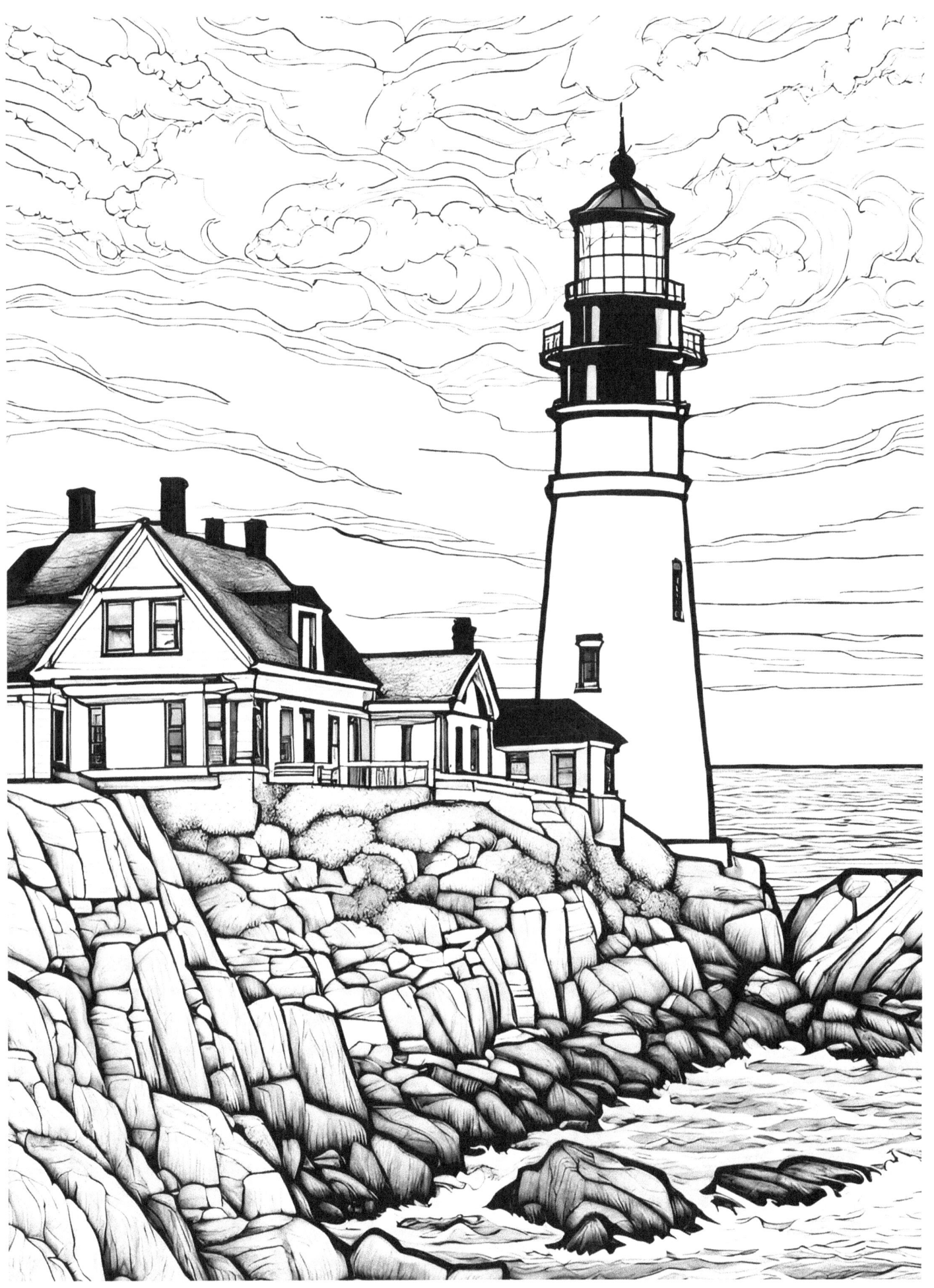

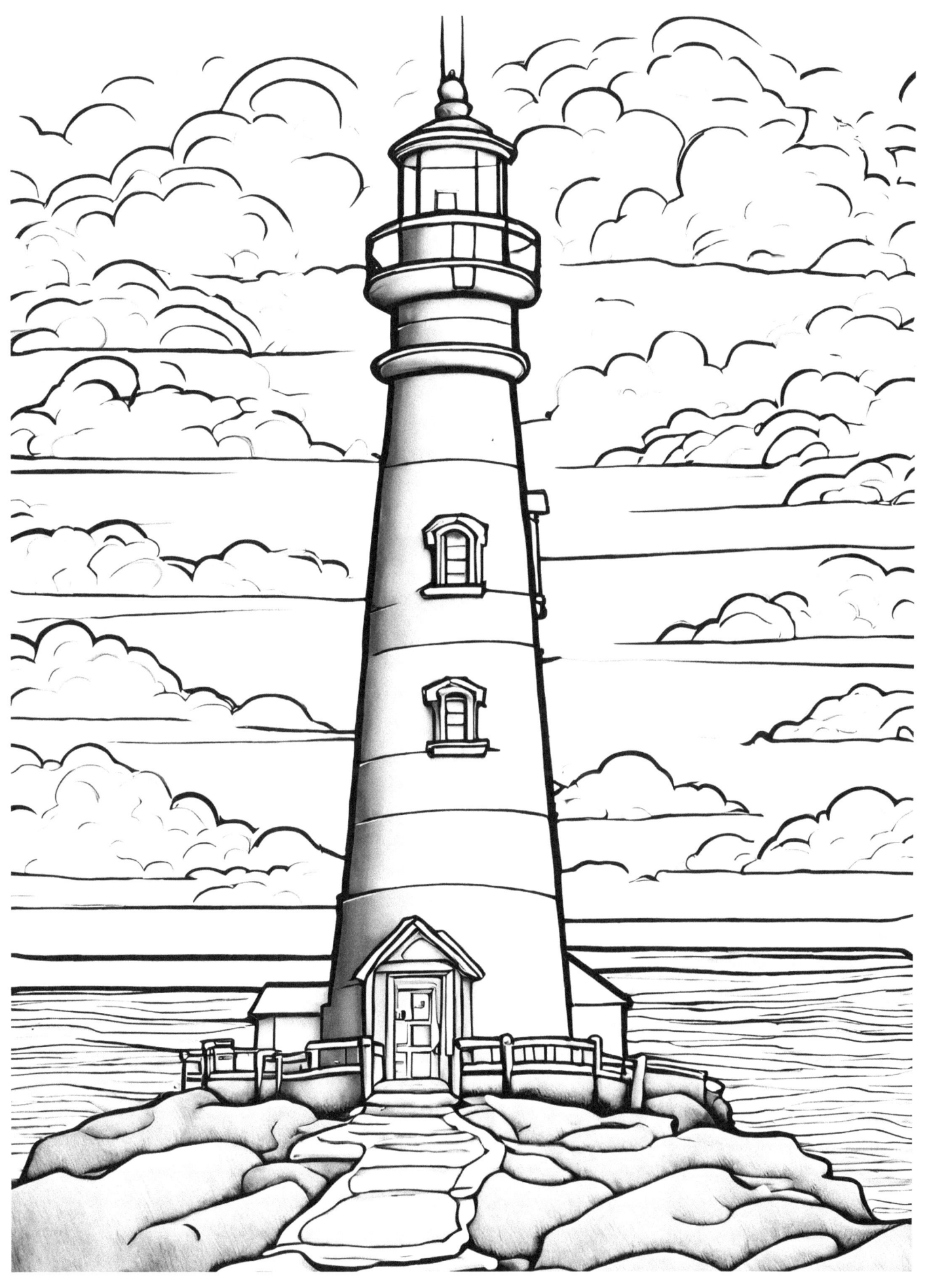

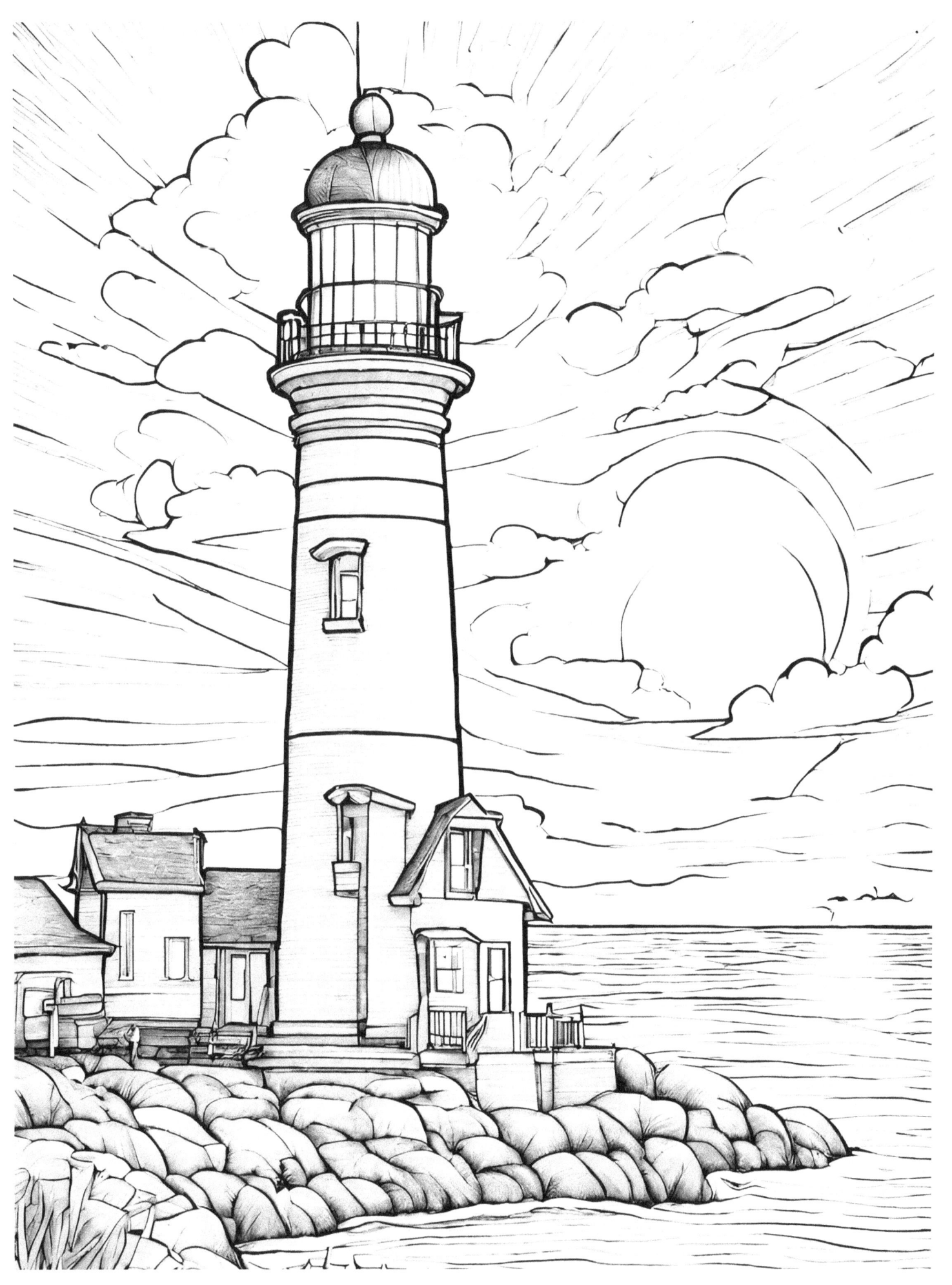

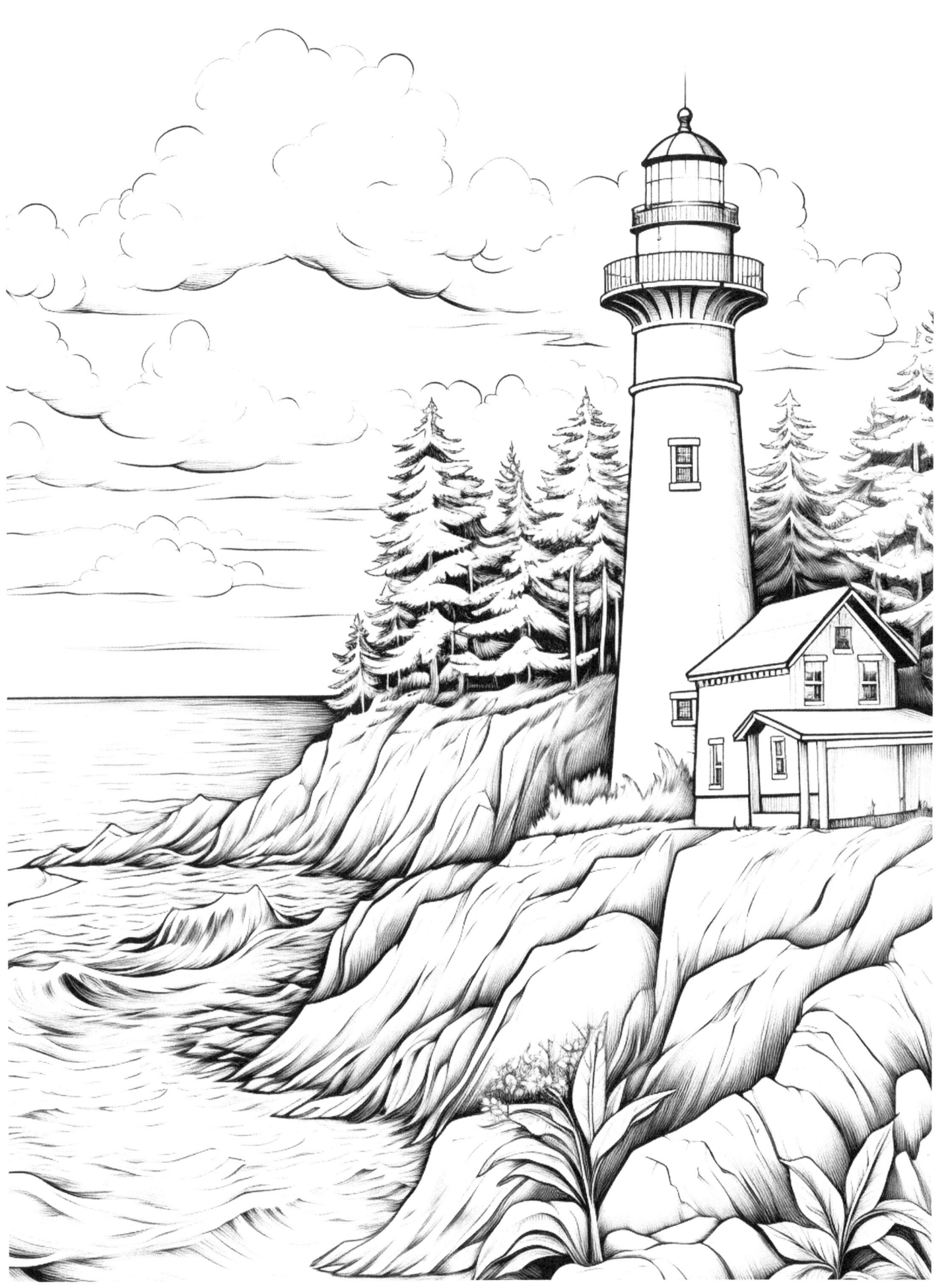

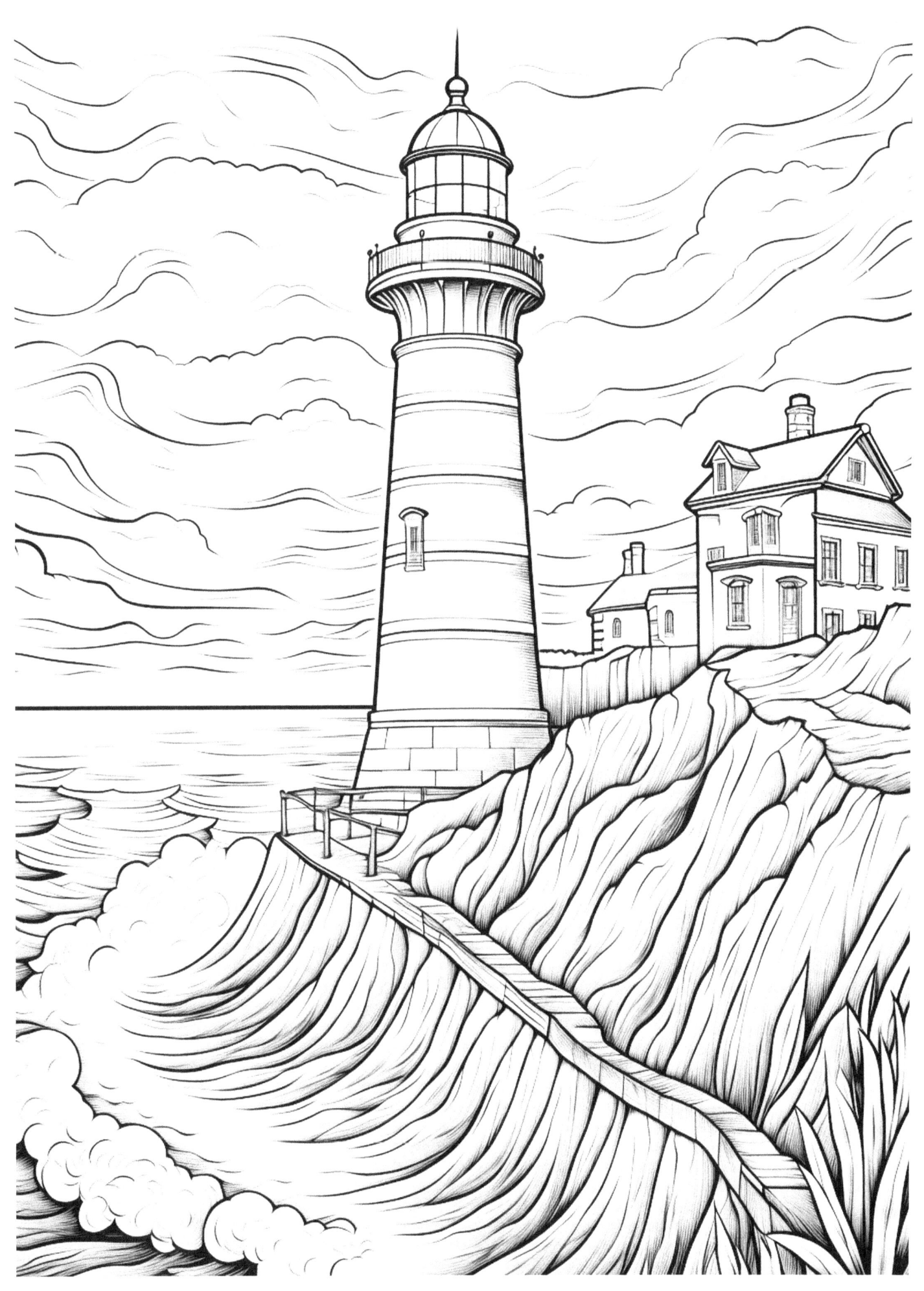

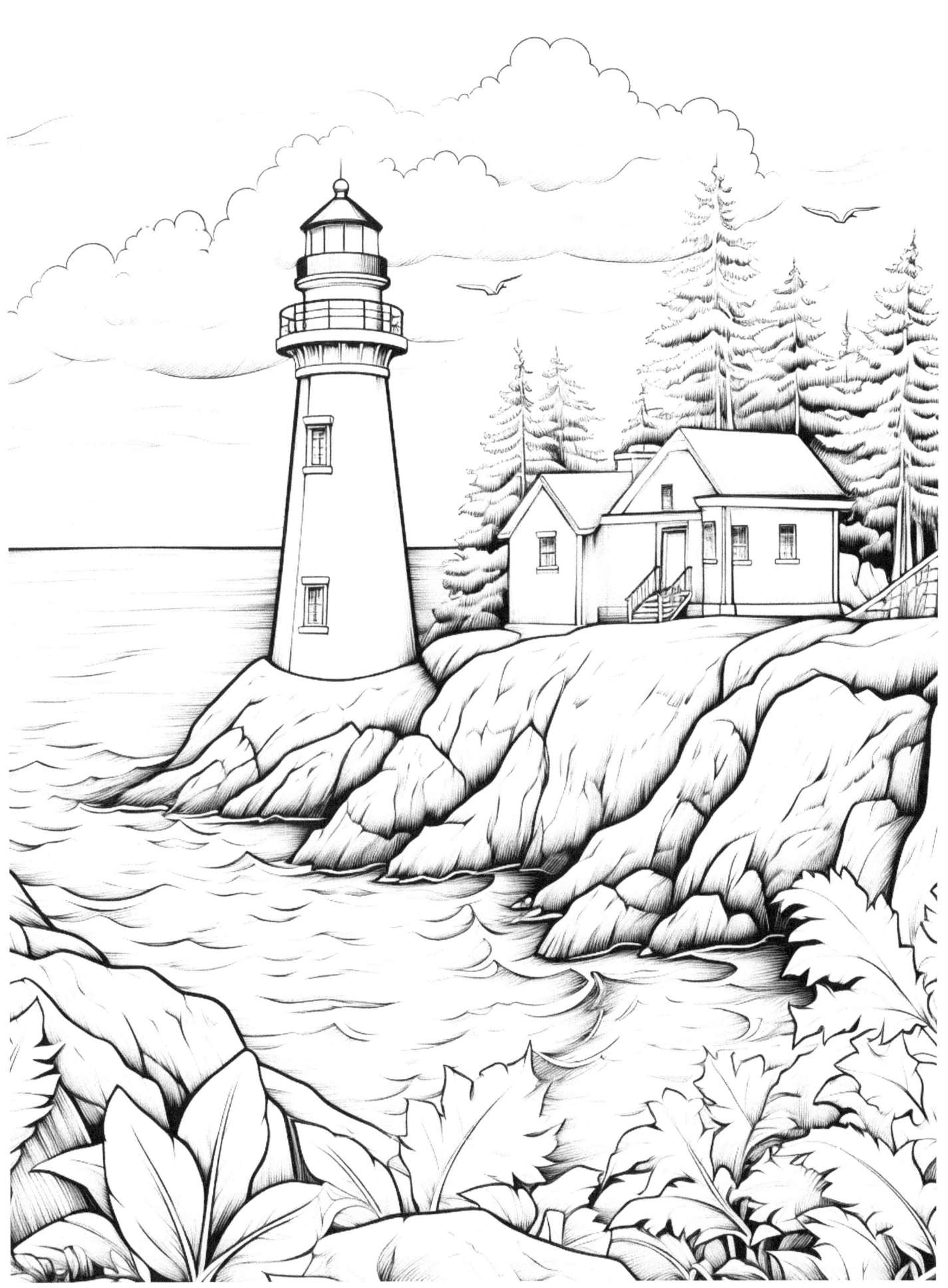

A Special Thank You!

Dear Customer,

I hope this message finds you well! I wanted to take a moment to express my sincere gratitude for your recent purchase of my Lighthouse Seascapes coloring book. Your support means the world to me, and I'm thrilled that my creations have found a place in your world of creativity. I hope it brings you joy, relaxation, and countless moments of inspiration.

I hope you've enjoyed the coloring book, I would be immensely grateful if you could take a few moments to share your thoughts with others by leaving a positive review. Your feedback not only helps me understand what you loved about the book but also assists potential customers in making informed decisions.

To leave a review, simply visit https://www.amazon.com/review/create-review/?ie=UTF8&channel=glance-detail&asin=B0CMDC7WXC on Amazon for my coloring book. Your words have the power to make a significant impact on the success of my small business, and I truly appreciate your support.

Once again, thank you for choosing my coloring book. If you have any questions or if there's anything else I can do for you, please don't hesitate to reach out. Your satisfaction is my top priority.
Wishing you many colorful and joyful moments ahead!

Sincerely,
Corinne Larsen
Email: larsenbcsales@gmail.com